The National Board Certification® Workbook

SECOND EDITION

The National Board Certification® Workbook

How to Develop Your Portfolio and Prepare for the Assessment Exams

SECOND EDITION

Adrienne Mack-Kirschner

HEINEMANN
Portsmouth, NH

Heinemann
A division of Reed Elsevier Inc.
361 Hanover Street
Portsmouth, NH 03801–3912
www.heinemann.com

Offices and agents throughout the world

Library of Congress Cataloging-in-Publication Data
Mack-Kirschner, Adrienne, 1944–
    The National Board certification workbook : how to develop your portfolio and prepare for the assessment exams / Adrienne Mack-Kirschner.— 2nd ed.
        p. cm.
    Includes bibliographical references.
    ISBN 0-325-00787-X
    1. Teachers—Certification—United States—Handbooks, manuals, etc.
2. Education—Standards—United States—Handbooks, manuals, etc. I. Title.

LB1771.M25 2005
371.12—dc22
2004023101

Editor: Lois Bridges
Production coordinator: Elizabeth Valway
Production service: Argosy
Cover design: Jenny Jensen Greenleaf
Cover photography: Steve Bernier
Composition: Argosy
Manufacturing: Steve Bernier

Printed in the United States of America on acid-free paper
09 08   ML   4 5

Contents

Introduction

Staff development is something that is done to you.

Professional development is something you do for yourself.

The National Board for Professional Teaching Standards® (NBPTS) is the highest and most comprehensive professional development experience you can give yourself. Although your initial goal may be to achieve certification on your first attempt, to gain access to financial incentives, or to attain a promotion you desire, once you have completed the portfolio and the assessment center exercises you will agree with thousands of other teachers in saying that the professional growth you've experienced, the personal renewal, was its own reward. *The journey is the destination.*

Whether you are a candidate yourself or a support provider for teacher-candidates, follow along the pages of this interactive workbook, which will guide you as you examine your teaching practices and prepare for National Board (NB) Certification.® This newly revised edition reflects the work I do supporting NB candidates, over 1,000 pre-K–12 teachers in the past 8 years! In this edition I've incorporated the latest NB changes and most up-to-date information. I've responded to questions and concerns that candidates have repeatedly identified. And I've emphasized and strengthened the information for areas in which teachers have struggled the most in the past.

The companion book, *The Teacher's Guide to National Board Certification: Unpacking the Standards,* will deepen candidates' knowledge about the core propositions underlying all of the certificate-specific standards. Although it is not mandatory to begin with the guide before advancing to the workbook, it is strongly recommended. The guide also serves as a valuable text for professional discussions about accomplished teaching and learning. As a prerequisite to the year-long support program, my NB candidates participate in two precandidate workshops during which we study the core propositions as presented in the *Teacher's Guide* and respond to what those propositions look like in our teaching practices. Following the precandidate study sessions, some teachers determine they need more time to improve their practice and delay beginning their candidate year, whereas others are empowered through identifying their strengths and know the time is right to begin their candidacy.

THE WORKBOOK OUTCOMES

This revised workbook begins with the basics: who is eligible for certification; how to apply; where to get the instructions, standards, and scoring guides. We quickly visit the five core propositions. (The core propositions are the essence of the *Teacher's Guide*.) We then *walk through* the massive portfolio instructions, over 225 pages, breaking them down into manageable and useable parts you'll refer to throughout your candidacy. We'll examine the NB standards and take personal inventories that help you to examine where and how your practice reflects the NB core propositions and the certificate-specific standards. Your classroom environment promotes learning, or it doesn't; it's the foundation for the learning that happens. We write the contextual information, the big picture (school and district), of your teaching environment.

We then continue by examining Entries 1, 2, and 3 in depth and do an overview of all three entries so you can plan ahead. These entries are based on student work, so studying Knowing Our Students comes next. Next are instructions for writing the Instructional Context of your teaching practice—the instructional snapshot. The next chapters address instructional goals and the strategies you select to help students to meet those goals. The workbook supplements the excellent NB instructions on videotaping. There's some discussion around analyzing student work and providing feedback, followed by exercises to complete Entry 4, "Documented Accomplishments."

Although writing style is not a separate standard, communicating your ideas clearly and concisely is important. You'll find a chapter on writing. We'll leave the portfolio entries there, spend a little time on the assessment center exercises, and then examine scoring, focusing on the scoring rubrics. After that we prepare a graphic organizer and consider a time line.

I strongly urge you to surround yourself with supportive colleagues and to form a cohort group in which you can examine and critique one another's portfolio work. Teachers have worked in isolation far too long. You'll find a recommended protocol for examining one another's work (which you can also adapt for your classroom) and some reflective conversation starters you may use when working together.

Think about your teaching, plan and deliver, gather your data, analyze and write, and then pack and ship. Chapter 20 offers some quick dos and don'ts for packing and shipping.

This workbook, in addition to serving as your guide to completing the portfolio and preparing for the assessment center, also suggests some effective strategies that enable you to demonstrate best student-centered classroom practice, but because it's a workbook, we can only mention those strategies here. For a more comprehensive guide to effective teaching where students monitor and manage their own learning, establish cooperative learning environments, maintain portfolios, conduct student-led conferences, and acquire 21st-century skills, consult my newly released: *Straight Talk for Today's Teachers*.

I thank you for joining me on this important professional journey.

Respectfully,

Adrienne Mack-Kirschner, Ed.D.
National Board Certified Teacher®

The National Board Certification® Workbook

SECOND EDITION

 # NUTS AND BOLTS

HOW TO ACHIEVE CERTIFICATION

To become a National Board Certified Teacher (NBCT®) practitioners must provide *clear, convincing,* and *consistent* evidence they have met the NB standards at an accomplished level. You show accomplishment by completing four portfolio entries and successfully taking six 30-minute grade- and content-specific examinations. The four portfolio entries, worth 60 percent of the final score, and the six exams, worth 40 percent of the final score, together comprise the requirements. A total score of 275 of a possible 400 points is necessary for certification. The NB sets the bar high, but not unattainably so. The scores are flexible, cumulative because you may have more strength in some areas than in others, and bankable for three years. More about scoring in a later chapter.

Three portfolio entries are based on student work, classroom videos, and other instructional artifacts. The fourth entry is about the work you do and have done to advance your professional learning, what you do to engage parents and the community as learning partners, and your collegial collaborations. The six assessment center exams concentrate on your content and grade-level knowledge. With everything you do for this certificate, the focus is always on student learning. The questions guiding you as you complete the portfolio entries will in themselves enrich your teaching practice.

CHECK YOUR ELIGIBILITY

- [ ] Baccalaureate degree from an accredited institution
- [ ] Completion of three years of successful teaching (or counseling for counseling certificate) of students pre-K–12
- [ ] Valid state teaching (counseling) license for each of those three years (Conditions apply where no state teaching or counseling license is required. Check with NBPTS.)

WHICH CERTIFICATE IS RIGHT FOR YOU

The National Board offers certificates for most classroom teachers, library media specialists, and counselors. The certificate you apply for should match your current teaching situation. Your choice depends on your teaching duties not on your credential or major field of past college study. For example, you may have a math degree, but if you teach a self-contained first-grade class, your certificate is most likely the Early Childhood Generalist, not the math specialist. However, you may have some additional choices. Do you teach English Language Learners? Students with exceptional needs? Are you an itinerant teacher? Do you specialize in art or music? You may be eligible for more than one certificate. Do a quick check of the available certificates by reading the overviews for any certificates you are considering (i.e., English as a New Language or Early Childhood Generalist). You can read the certificate overviews online at www.nbpts.org/candidates/guide/2_certglance.html.

Note that the ages of 51 percent of your students during your candidacy year may affect your certificate choice.

LOW-DEMAND CERTIFICATES

The National Board's goal is to provide certification opportunities for all teachers. Regrettably, it has had to withdraw several low-demand certificates. If yours is one of them, Health Education for example, contact your professional organization to rally a significant number of members who might collectively petition the NB to reopen these low-demand certificates.

PORTFOLIO INSTRUCTIONS, NB STANDARDS, SCORING GUIDE

All of the documents are available for viewing or printing without charge, even before you apply to be a candidate. You can access these documents at www.nbpts.org/candidates/ckc.cfm. These are large files. The instructions are upward of 225 pages, the standards are approximately 100 pages, and the scoring guide another 60. Depending upon the capacity of your printer, you may find that downloading and printing the materials is best done in small batches. Once you have downloaded the materials, I recommend that you put the instructions into one 2-inch binder and the standards and scoring guide into a second, smaller binder. You will be using these materials extensively throughout your candidacy year.

After you apply for candidacy and send your $300 nonrefundable application fee, you receive a portfolio box with a bound standards booklet and a CD-ROM that includes the portfolio instructions. Although you may have already downloaded the standards, it is worthwhile to have two sets—one for home and another to reference at school. Make the standards your companion.

All of the portfolio entries, as well as the assessment center exercises, must be typed. At the very least you should be comfortable negotiating an electronic text document. I estimate that accurately typing 45 words or more, at a minimum, enables you to focus on the entries without worrying about the mechanics. In the future, portfolio entries will be electronically submitted. Already, with few exceptions, the assessment center option of handwriting has been eliminated. And this is how it should be. If we are to prepare our students for successful participation in the 21st century, technology should be part of our practice. A teacher's comfort with basic computer functions—text documents, spreadsheets, e-mail, and the Internet—at minimum, transfers to students.

With each revision of the standards there is a greater emphasis on effectively incorporating technology into your practice. If you need this year to become more computer savvy, it will be a year well spent. Certification can wait until you're ready.

ORGANIZATION

Save yourself a great deal of grief by getting organized early. Put your instructions, standards, and scoring guide into binders. Get a box (standard cardboard storage box works fine, or a plastic crate available at any stationery store) and label it. Use hanging files to separate each entry, study notes, student work samples, permission forms, and any other documents you may need. When you receive your official portfolio box and labels, you can save them there as well. You will need to return your entries in the box provided by the National Board—do not discard it!

REFLECTIVE JOURNAL

Select a bound notebook you can use as a journal. In my experience the basic reasons teachers do not complete the process or, once completed, do not certify following their first attempt are because of their ineffective time management and/or their inability to reflect deeply on their practice. If reflection is not a part of your regular practice—and no one faults you if it is not, given the hectic, nonstop nature of the teaching day—begin now. Included throughout the workbook are suggestions for reflection on your practice.

Use the notebook to record those *a-ha* moments when you have a revelation, when something amazing happens in your classroom, and when you just don't want to forget a conversation with a parent or student or colleague. Your reflective journal will be a valuable resource as you compile your portfolio entries. The more you are in the habit of reflecting on your practice, the easier it will be to complete the portfolio and to learn from the experience. You are more likely to achieve certification if you can "wrap your mind around your teaching." If you are unable to set aside some of your other interests and really concentrate on your teaching practice, certification will be difficult to attain.

BACKWARD DESIGN

The National Board uses the best standards-based instructional strategies in outlining the portfolio requirements. At the onset teacher-candidates know the specific standards for each certificate, the scoring guides by which their entries will be assessed, and the complete instructions for each portfolio entry. How does this structure compare to your teaching practice? Do students know in advance the standards they are expected to meet? Do they have a scoring guide specifying the criteria by which their accomplishments will be measured? Are your instructions to them clearly communicated and easy to follow?

FOLLOW THE PORTFOLIO INSTRUCTIONS—EXACTLY

I can't emphasize enough how important it is to read carefully and to follow the instructions. All of your portfolio entry documents must be formatted with 1-inch margins on all four sides. Only Times New Roman font in 12 point size is acceptable. When the instructions recommend a page count, although only a recommendation, it is a good practice to respond within the recommended number of pages. My general rule of thumb is that you should not vary from the suggested page allowance by more than 10 percent. If your response is either 10 percent longer or 10 percent shorter than recommended, you've written more than necessary or not enough to fully respond to the prompt, so consider revising. When the instructions include a maximum page allowance, you may not exceed the page length—your extra page(s) will not be read! Videotaping instructions vary with each certificate, so study your own. Videotapes are unedited. Follow your certificate instructions exactly.

APPLICATION

You may complete your entire NB application online using a credit card for payment. Because the initial $300 is nonrefundable once you apply, I suggest that before you apply you study the core propositions and at least complete the standards inventories included in this workbook. Once you understand the depth of the standards and the expectations for demonstration of accomplished teaching, you are in a better position to determine whether this is the correct time to begin your candidacy.

Before you apply to the NB, check your state and local district to ascertain whether either one or both offer fee support. Apply for all available scholarships; you apply for scholarships online through the NB website after you are an official candidate. Additional scholarships may be available through your local Rotary or other service club, from your religious organization, or through your local teachers' union. Low-cost loans are available through the National Educators Association (NEA) and American Federation of Teachers (AFT). You can access these online through the NB website.

You may apply any time during the year. All portfolios are due in the spring. Check the NB website for exact dates because they may vary from year to year.

FIVE CORE PROPOSITIONS

All of the certificate standards are based on the five core propositions:

1. Teachers are committed to students and their learning.
2. Teachers know the subjects they teach and how to teach those subjects to students.
3. Teachers are responsible for managing and monitoring student learning.
4. Teachers think systematically about their practice and learn from their experience.
5. Teachers are members of learning communities.

The full text for each of the propositions is available on the NBPTS website; the propositions are also included with each set of portfolio instructions. Read them, analyze them, think about them, visualize how they appear in the most accomplished practice, and then rate your teaching against them. An in-depth analysis of each proposition is the heart of *The Teacher's Guide to National Board Certification: Unpacking the Standards,* already mentioned in the introduction. I strongly encourage you to read through the *Teacher's Guide* and to complete the reflective exercises. You will be better prepared for the work ahead if you have a strong foundation and understand the big picture that governs all of the National Board work.

If you have not studied the *Teacher's Guide,* then complete the following exercises:

INSTRUCTIONS

- ☐ Use the personal inventory sheets appearing on the following pages as you examine your practice against the NB core propositions. A sample inventory is provided. Duplicate pages as needed.
- ☐ For each core proposition, while you read, highlight the key ideas as you understand them. Don't be surprised if your colleagues highlight different key ideas. The propositions are very complex. Each time I study them, depending upon where I am in my professional work, I find other significant key points; you may find the same.

☐ Provide one or more specific examples of how this key idea looks in your practice. I've provided some examples.

☐ Note how you might strengthen your practice.

☐ Write down the steps you will take to become a more accomplished teacher.

PERSONAL INVENTORY SHEET—EXAMPLE

Core Proposition 1: Teachers Are Committed to Students and Their Learning

KEY POINTS	CLEAR, CONSISTENT, AND CONVINCING EVIDENCE	POSSIBLE IMPROVEMENTS	NEXT STEPS
All students can learn.	I assess each child's current skill level to determine how best to help the child continue learning.	I could know more about how the brain learns.	Study *How People Learn*, from the National Research Council. Encourage a colleague to study how the brain works with me.
Make knowledge accessible.	I build on what students already know and add incrementally to their existing knowledge. I use strategies such as KWL and reciprocal teaching to enhance learning.	I could examine how I give instructions to make certain they are clear and accessible to all students.	Write out the instructions and ask a group of students to read them and provide feedback to me so I can improve my practice.
Students' lives have dignity.	I value students' home cultures and believe they each bring something of value to the classroom. Our classroom has a bulletin board with photos the students take of their neighborhoods.	Project: Get disposable cameras so all students can take out-of-school pictures of their lives beyond the playground. Use these for talking points about cultural differences and similarities.	Investigate small grants to cover the cost of cameras for students. Contact PTA.
Pay attention to variability between students.	Students are unique. Each is valued. When we write poetry, students select their own topics to write about.	Include more ways students can demonstrate accomplishment instead of the one or two options I usually provide. Concentrate on more differentiated instruction.	Check with other teachers about how they provide differentiated instruction and multiple assessments.

© 2005 by Adrienne Mack-Kirschner from *The National Board Certification Workbook*, Second Edition, Portsmouth, NH: Heinemann

PERSONAL INVENTORY WORKSHEETS

Core Proposition 1: Teachers Are Committed to Students and Their Learning

KEY POINTS	CLEAR, CONSISTENT, AND CONVINCING EVIDENCE	POSSIBLE IMPROVEMENTS	NEXT STEPS

(Duplicate as needed.) © 2005 by Adrienne Mack-Kirschner from *The National Board Certification Workbook*, Second Edition, Portsmouth, NH: Heinemann

Core Proposition 2: Teachers Know the Subjects They Teach and How to Teach Those Subjects to Students

Key Points	Clear, Consistent, and Convincing Evidence	Possible Improvements	Next Steps

Core Proposition 3: Teachers Are Responsible for Managing and Monitoring Student Learning

Key Points	Clear, Consistent, and Convincing Evidence	Possible Improvements	Next Steps

(Duplicate as needed.) © 2005 by Adrienne Mack-Kirschner from *The National Board Certification Workbook*, Second Edition, Portsmouth, NH: Heinemann

Core Proposition 4: Teachers Think Systematically About Their Practice and Learn from Experience

Key Points	Clear, Consistent, and Convincing Evidence	Possible Improvements	Next Steps

(Duplicate as needed.) © 2005 by Adrienne Mack-Kirschner from *The National Board Certification Workbook*, Second Edition, Portsmouth, NH: Heinemann

Core Proposition 5: Teachers Are Members of Learning Communities

Key Points	Clear, Consistent, and Convincing Evidence	Possible Improvements	Next Steps

A WALK THROUGH THE
PORTFOLIO INSTRUCTIONS

The portfolio instructions is a massive document that candidates tell me is intimidating even before they begin to read it. But once we go through it and divide it into workable chunks, the mystery is gone and the documents become user friendly.

With the instructions at your side, follow along as we walk through the document. To take this stroll it's best if you have the instructions already in a binder, have access to an ample supply of dividers and sticky notes, and have one or more colored highlighters. I'll indicate where it's valuable to have a divider, sticky note, or to highlight for easy reference. Of course, if something else jumps off the page that you want to remember or examine further, mark that as well.

INTRODUCTION [DIVIDER]

☐ Overview of the certificate. Remember that 51 percent of your students must be within the stated age range for the certificate [highlight this] and that "you may collect evidence for 12 months prior to your portfolio due date." If your portfolio is due at the end of March, for example, you may collect evidence beginning April 1 in the prior year. This is especially important when it comes to contact with parents that may overlap more than one school year, but still be within the 12 months. More about this when we get to Entry 4.

☐ 5 Core Propositions. [Divider] These are covered in Chapter 2. The full text is included in the instructions. If you haven't already read and studied the core propositions, don't miss this opportunity to identify the key points and to complete the inventory against your current practice (Chapter 2). Be sure to read the concluding statements following the five core propositions.

☐ More detailed Overview. [sticky note]
  • The three types of entries
  • Entry directions

- Scoring
  - Guidelines: Read carefully and highlight [sticky note]

☐ Completing Portfolio Forms. There are lots and lots of forms. These repeat for each of the three entries that highlight student work and again for part of Entry 4. Yes, you are seeing the same forms again and again. Use them exactly as they are provided in the instructions. Get the student and adult release forms completed as soon as possible and put them into your organizing box. You will not be sending them to the National Board; you keep them and send a letter (another form) stating that you have them on file. These adult and student release forms are signed only once.

☐ Collaboration. We love collaboration and encourage it. However, [highlight] "all of the work you submit as part of your response to any entry must be yours and yours alone." You can plan together and deliver the same lesson(s) to different groups of students, but the work you collect must be a direct result of your teaching.

☐ Additional Considerations. These include references to Spanish language options and nonstandard accommodations (primarily for the assessment center).

☐ Verification Forms. Complete these forms as soon after you apply as possible. Keep them simple. Your school/district already has your education and work record on file, so there is no need, in most cases, to obtain your transcript. A current administrator or office assistant can check your employee file to verify eligible past teaching experience. For most candidates, the single-page form is all that is required.

GET STARTED [DIVIDER]

This section includes tips for studying the standards (Chapter 4) and some examples for writing your entries, which we will also do elsewhere in this workbook. The writing examples included with the instructions are unscored and may not be helpful.

☐ Practice Activities. [sticky note] Includes some questions you might find helpful later on.

☐ Tips for Videotaping. [divider] This section is worth reading when you are ready to consider videotaping. The workbook chapter on videotaping includes tips and information not found in the instructions; they are a supplement, not a replacement, for the information in the instructions. The Analysis Questions [sticky note] also supplement those included in this workbook and are worth considering as you review your videotapes and before you decide which tapes to submit.

☐ Cover Sheets and Forms. [sticky note] You'll get the forms again and again. Refer back to this section as needed.

Formatting is covered here, again. There's lots of duplication in the instructions, hence the size. The NB has attempted to provide all of the information necessary especially for candidates who do not have the benefit of a knowledgeable support provider. This attempt to be thorough sometimes causes confusion because of the duplication and wordiness. This walk-through should demystify the instructions.

Portfolio-Related Terms [divider]

This is an important section you should definitely read and use. Remember that the NB certification process is a national program. Terms and acronyms that your school/district uses locally may be used differently on the national level, or not used at all. Always use the terms as they are used in this glossary; that's how the assessors will understand them. There is a thorough explanation of what constitutes student work [highlight]; follow it.

Be careful about your use of acronyms. The first time you name an organization, program, or idea that has an acronym, write it out in full, followed by the acronym in parentheses. For subsequent references, you can then use the acronym only.

Follow the same procedure when you define a system, a program, or something you are doing at your site or in your district that may not be universally applicable. For instance, the first time I mentioned "The university department in which teaching practice and research intersected," in my portfolio entry on documented accomplishments. I wrote Center X in parentheses. In subsequent references I used Center X only. Note, I didn't put the name of the university because the portfolio instructions ask that we avoid using identifying names whenever possible.

- ☐ Planning and Time Management. It is critically important that you create and maintain a realistic schedule for when you will complete your portfolio entries. You'll find useful tips in this workbook in Chapter 19: Time Management.
- ☐ Communication Log. [sticky note] This is a recommendation, not a requirement. Some candidates complain that the log doesn't allow for two-way communication, even though the board expects it. I have adapted the form to indicate who initiated the contact to best demonstrate that the teacher has a partnership with parents and other significant adults. I also suggest that you include any *next steps* you might take to complete the communication. The fifth column is for Impact on Student(s). This is information you will want to have when you complete Documented Accomplishments, Entry 4. You may duplicate this log as needed.

COMMUNICATION LOG

DATE	CONTACT INITIATED BY:	TYPE OF COMMUNICATION (TELEPHONE, WRITTEN, E-MAIL, IN PERSON)	NATURE OF COMMUNICATION (REASON FOR COMMUNICATION, OUTCOME OF COMMUNICATION, NEXT STEPS—IF ANY)	IMPACT ON STUDENT(S)

(Duplicate as needed) © 2005 by Adrienne Mack-Kirschner from *The National Board Certification Workbook*, Second Edition, Portsmouth, NH: Heinemann

- [ ] Entry Tracking Form. [sticky note] You may find this helpful to keep track of which students you used for which entry.
- [ ] Time Requirements. I think this is unrealistic. Most candidates benefit from more time, not the five months indicated here. My candidates work for 8 to 10 months after they complete the precandidate workshops. You'll find another timeline in Chapter 19.
- [ ] Summary. [sticky note] Useful for doing your backward planning.
- [ ] Additional Resources. [sticky note] Uniform Resource Locators (URLs) for contacting the board.

ENTRY 1 [DIVIDER]

- [ ] Overview. [highlight]
- [ ] What you need to do. Note the page allowances and other requirements. [highlight specific requirements]
- [ ] Scoring. It is worth reading the level 4 rubric and then checking your draft entry against the rubric. This will enable you to make changes to better address the requirements as you revise. [highlight key points in the rubric as you read]
- [ ] Instructions. [sticky note] Read and follow the instructions carefully as you begin each entry, and then again after you write your first draft, and then again. Some candidates do not certify because they do not follow the directions, or they don't answer parts of the prompts, or they make incorrect assumptions and omit what they should include. Follow the instructions. Keep it simple.
- [ ] Making Good Choices. [sticky note] Good suggestions, worth reading, including how to select students and work to feature.
- [ ] Format Specifications. Yet again.
- [ ] Student Responses. [sticky note] [highlight key points] Follow the directions.
- [ ] Cover sheets and forms. Use them as indicated even though there appears to be significant duplication. There are many forms, each with a specific purpose. The bar codes indicating your candidate number (that's why you don't need to include your name) are included in the portfolio box you receive after you apply to the NB. Save them in your organization crate because you will need them when you pack and ship your portfolio entries.
- [ ] Contextual Information Sheet. [sticky note] We'll discuss this at length in Chapter 6: The Big Picture.

ENTRY 2 AND ENTRY 3 [DIVIDERS]

These entries follow the same format as Entry 1 and can be divided, noted, and highlighted in a similar fashion. Although the format is the same in each entry, the substance, what you are asked to do, varies.

ENTRY 4 [DIVIDER]

The instructions follow the same format as the preceding three entries. We will be discussing this entry at length in Chapter 14: Documented Accomplishments.

PACKING AND SHIPPING [DIVIDER]

This section includes explicit instructions for packing and shipping that you will need later. This is where you will find information on where to apply the bar codes, how to assemble, whether you can staple (do not bend, fold, or mutilate), and any other information you need for packing and shipping. The National Board even supplies diagrams to follow.

ADDITIONAL MATERIALS [DIVIDER]

Certificate instructions vary at this point. Some provide student content standards, big ideas in science, or other supplemental material. If instructions are there, it is most likely helpful to read through them before you begin your entries. Not all certificates include supplemental materials.

CONCLUDING STATEMENT [DIVIDER]

By now, if you have been using the workbook as your guide while we explore the portfolio instructions, the mystery is gone, the huge volume of paper has become manageable, and you know where to go to get what you need during your candidacy.

4 EXAMINING THE NATIONAL BOARD CERTIFICATE STANDARDS

Now it's time for a very personal inventory against the NB certificate standards. We'll use the same technique we used for examining the core propositions, only these standards represent accomplished teaching in your grade level and field. Just as in the core propositions, the standards overlap. You'll find key points in one that are similar to key points in another. You be the judge of how detailed you want this inventory to be. The more preparation and self-analysis you do now, the easier it will be to analyze your teaching later on. Remember that to achieve National Board Certification you must provide *clear, convincing,* and *consistent* evidence that you have met the standards at an accomplished level. The better you know the standards, the more you have absorbed what they say, what they mean, and why they matter, the better choices you'll make as you complete the portfolio entries and the greater the improvement in and awareness of your own teaching.

Time spent reading and reflecting on the standards is time well spent. As you highlight the key points in each standard, closely examine the language of the standards. Pay attention to the active verbs. Highlight them. As you teach, reflect upon the standards. Are you meeting them? Are there gaps you need to fill? Can you stretch what you're currently doing to move more deeply into accomplished teaching? Weave the language of the standards throughout your entry as you write.

Complete an individual inventory for each standard in your certificate. The examples included on the following pages are offered as a guide only, not required strategies for your practice. Whenever possible, show, don't tell. Get used to writing in concrete rather than abstract images. Once you submit your portfolio, you will not be able to explain to the assessors orally anything that you might have omitted from your written commentary. Therefore, it is critical that your written work is clear and concise, that you *show* your practice. Duplicate the inventory forms as needed.

Some teachers become very defensive while completing these personal inventories. They have a way of teaching they're comfortable with and resent when someone or something suggests there is another way. I am convinced, as are many other educators, that because the National Board has had extensive input from classroom teachers during the development of the standards that these standards do represent best teaching practices. There is, however, an underlying philosophy that appears to permeate all of them.

First, there is an assumption that the classroom is student-centered, and second, that your practice is progressive, ever evolving to meet the needs of the 21st century, not just repeating what and how we've taught in the past.

If, as you examine these standards and measure your practice against them, you find a particular area that causes you discomfort, or with which you absolutely disagree, that's a great place to stop for reflection or to join with colleagues in discussion. In my experience, teachers who provide a rationale for why they are teaching a particular subject, or for the strategies they choose to help students meet the instructional goals, have the same opportunity to certify as teachers selecting other goals and strategies. Although there are standards, the interpretation and practice vary greatly. There is room for you here.

Keep in mind that the National Board standards are for accomplished teachers and will differ significantly in their depth and breadth from the standards for new teachers many of us are familiar with in our work as mentors and coaches. The National Board has raised the standards for the profession. How do you measure up? Where do you need to stretch and grow?

I have included some graphic organizers to help you to think about your practice as it relates to each standard. The examples provided in the following chart represent a limited demonstration of teaching practice and are offered only as models for how you might think and write about your practice. You will not be submitting these graphic organizers with your portfolio. They are included to assist you as you examine the standards and how your practice matches those standards. They are also good practice in thinking concretely and identifying actions you take or can take to meet the standards.

These are the directions for using the graphic organizer:

☐ Key points. Select those ideas from the standards that you consider critical at this time. Briefly note them in the first column.

☐ *Clear, convincing, consistent* evidence. What are those behaviors that an observer will see/hear in your classroom practice?

☐ Possible improvements. If you are unable to find strong evidence of this key point in your current practice, what might you do differently? What might you do more consistently? What practices might you discontinue? And why?

☐ Next steps. Try to identify steps you can take to strengthen your practice as it reflects this standard. We are more likely to improve if we set clear, specific, and timely goals.

Standards Inventory Sheet—Example

Certificate: Middle Childhood Generalist   Standard: 1. Knowledge of Students

KEY POINTS	CLEAR, CONSISTENT, AND CONVINCING EVIDENCE	POSSIBLE IMPROVEMENTS	NEXT STEPS
Student diversity is an asset.	Our word wall has a column for targeted English Language words and columns for the same word/concept in students' native languages. One year I had 6 columns to represent the diverse students in class.	I might also do some charting of corresponding cultures that represent who is in our class.	Early in the semester identify the cultural background of each student and learn something about the various cultures.
MC begins to consider perspectives other than their own.	I teach point of view using the story "The Three Little Pigs" and the "Real Story of the Three Little Pigs as Told by A. Wolff."	Include more ways of understanding one another's point of view, including on the playground.	Check with other MC teachers about how they address point of view and multiple perspectives.
Understand what students know.	Students don't come in with empty minds. I use the KWL strategy to assess what students already know about the upcoming unit/concepts.	Expand this strategy so I can also identify any misconceptions and address those. Might tie this in with point of view. Find out any special interests students have.	Study the content standards for the primary grades so I have a better understanding of what students have studied prior to coming to my class. Check with the teachers.
Address student inquisitiveness and energy.	I regularly mix up seat time with moving around time. Resources are open and available. I bring interesting things, such as bugs in jars, to class to explore.	With all the requirements, how can I maintain wonder and joy? Find out what students are doing and thinking at home. Talk to parents more.	Perhaps by studying the mandated curriculum more closely, I can find ways to supplement and to add movement, visuals, and surprises.

STANDARDS PERSONAL INVENTORY WORKSHEET

Certificate: _____   Standard: _____

KEY POINTS	CLEAR, CONSISTENT, AND CONVINCING EVIDENCE	POSSIBLE IMPROVEMENTS	NEXT STEPS

CLASSROOM ENVIRONMENT: AFFECTIVE AND EFFECTIVE

A learning space must be hospitable—inviting as well as open, safe and trustworthy, as well as free. . . . [It] must have features that help students deal with the dangers of an educational expedition: places to rest, places to find nourishment, even places to seek shelter when one feels overexposed.

—Parker Palmer, *The Courage to Teach*

I have had the privilege of working with hundreds of candidates over the past 8 years. I also observe in classrooms, talk and listen to teachers, mentor, and coach. Within a short time, 15 minutes or less, of focused observation I can tell a great deal about the teacher and the teaching—and so can the assessors. Although this is a workbook to assist you as you complete the National Board requirements, I thought it important to include some comments about classroom environment because it is such a critical part of your teaching. Few would disagree that where the classroom environment doesn't shout *I add value to all of my students,* certification is not likely to happen.

Establishing a classroom environment that supports learning, like the one Parker Palmer describes, takes time initially, but saves time over the course of the year. Whether we're establishing an inviting classroom environment that supports learning, getting to know the students in our classes, reading good literature, or examining the big ideas in science or social studies, we need to spend our time and resources on what we value the most. Spend some time to create and foster a learning community. Be mindful of your classroom environment in total, both the affective and the effective domains.

Here are some ideas to ponder:

- [ ] Meet them and greet them
  - Learn all students' names quickly
  - Greet them and welcome them to class daily
- [ ] Clean and green
  - Keep the room clean and attractive
  - Consider keeping live green plants donated by parents and students
- [ ] Sounds and smells
  - Consider playing background music
  - Keep room freshener handy
- [ ] Check your beliefs and biases
  - All kids can learn
- [ ] Question the rules—beginning with your own
  - Silence is not golden
- [ ] Life-long learning—begins with you
- [ ] Emotional safety—consider how you assure it
- [ ] Win-win atmosphere
- [ ] Celebrate
  - Everything
- [ ] Time
  - To think
  - To rejuvenate
  - To revise

Ours is an awesome responsibility. Teachers, to paraphrase Dr. Haim Ginott (*Between Teacher and Child*, 1972), are the decisive elements in their classrooms. They "possess a tremendous power to make a child's life miserable or joyous. . . . In all situations," it is the teacher's "response that decides whether a crisis will be escalated or deescalated, and a child humanized or dehumanized." For more detailed suggestions on creating a powerful classroom environment that supports learning, consult *Straight Talk for Today's Teachers: How to Teach so Students Learn*, Heinemann, 2005.

How you design your classroom, where the resources are, how accessible they are to students, where you locate your desk are all part of your classroom environment.

CLASSROOM LAYOUT AND LEARNING ENVIRONMENT

For each of the videotaped entries you will be asked to provide a sketch of your classroom layout. This is to enable the assessors to have a sense of the physical layout of your room. Take time to sketch your classroom layout as it is now. Include the position of student seating, activity centers, your desk, bookshelves, and other resources. Mark the location of windows and doors and anything else of significance in your room. You might want to use one color for things you can move and another for those that are in fixed positions.

Sketching your classroom as it exists has benefits beyond the assessors' needs. We often set up our classrooms without thinking about the implications of how student seating is arranged or where our desk is located. We sometimes don't consider the accessibility of resource materials and supplies. Reflecting on your current classroom layout is an excellent way to reflect on your teaching practice.

On pages 29–30 are some thoughts you might reflect on in your journal.

CLASSROOM LAYOUT

Sketch in your existing classroom layout.

Refer to reflective questions.

Reflection

1. How does my current classroom layout allow for student movement?

2. Student choice? Teacher movement? Group work? Access to resources? Other?

3. Does the room arrangement accommodate students with special needs?

Reflection

4. What does this layout imply about who has and does not have power and ownership?

5. How does this classroom layout support powerful teaching and learning?

Okay, you've reflected on how things are now, but because you've begun the certification process early, you have time to make changes in your classroom layout; you can create the environment you want and your students need.

Each certificate has standards related to the learning environment. Reread these standards now. Review your personal inventory, making additions or changes reflecting your current understanding. Revise your classroom layout using the following form. After you've done the new layout, refer to the preceding reflective questions and/or consider the reflection on page 33.

The reflective work you are doing here is not an exercise to complete and disregard. I wouldn't waste your valuable time; I know all too well how precious it is. The board is interested in your teaching choices and in why you have made those choices. The more you analyze why you do what you do, the more *clear, convincing,* and *consistent* your response and the more complete.

CLASSROOM LAYOUT REVISED

Sketch in your proposed/revised classroom layout.

Refer to reflective questions.

Reflection

1. Given the physical constraints of my classroom, why have I chosen to arrange the room the way I have?

2. How does this room arrangement contribute to student learning? How well does this arrangement allow for student access to materials and books?

3. Does the room arrangement allow for interaction between me and each student? Between students?

4. What further changes, if any, would best promote student and teacher learning?

6 CONTEXTUAL INFORMATION: THE BIG PICTURE

National Board Certification is not a competitive enterprise. There are no quotas limiting the number of teachers who can become certified. Teachers are not compared to one another with the *best* achieving certification and the *rest* left behind. All teacher-candidates who provide *clear*, *convincing*, and *consistent* evidence of meeting the standards achieve certification. Nevertheless, even though the standards are the same for all candidates in each certificate, there remain wide variations between teaching environments. The assessors are thoroughly familiar with the standards for the certificate they are scoring, but it is up to the individual candidate to provide an accurate picture of his or her professional environment for assessors to fairly score candidates' entries. The board seeks this information in two ways.

First, candidates are asked to describe the broader context in which they teach. Each entry includes a Contextual Information Sheet that asks you to identify your teaching context at the district and school level. Second, each entry includes instructions for describing the Instructional Context of the class featured in the specific entry. We consider the Instructional Context in Chapter 10. This chapter focuses on the Contextual Information Sheet—the big picture, a snapshot.

Find the Contextual Information Sheet in your instructions. One sheet is included in the forms section of each of the four entries. They are identical and need only be completed once, photocopied, and included with each entry if you teach in only one school.

Read the instructions at the top of the Contextual Information Sheet. In addition to the instructions provided in this workbook, the sheet provides instructions for teachers who teach in more than one school. You *must* use this form, responding in the space provided. This is the only place in the portfolio where you may single space your response; however, you still must use the 12 point Times New Roman font. Respond to the prompt for section 1 and for section 2. The prompts and responses that follow are examples only. You should consult the Contextual Information Sheet included with your portfolio instructions and respond to your prompts exactly.

Prompt 1. *Briefly identify the type of school/program in which you teach and the grade/subject configuration (single grade, departmentalized, interdisciplinary teams, etc.). Also identify the grade(s), age levels, courses, and number of students you teach each day, as well as the average number of students in each class.*

Sample Response: I teach in a year-round, multitrack urban comprehensive high school located on the fringe of a large city. The enrollment is 5,200 students in grades 9 through 12. The ethnic breakdown is as follows: 70% Hispanic, 12% African American, 9% Caucasian, 2% Native American, 3% Asian, and 4% other. Eighty percent of our students receive free or reduced lunch; 74% of the students are English Language Learners. The school is departmentalized by subject with no official interdisciplinary teams except for students enrolled in our magnet programs. The average class size is 30, but my ninth-grade classes are limited to 20 students each. I teach approximately 100 students daily.

Although candidates often worry about not having enough space for their responses, when you confine your response to what the prompt requests, you will be able to include all of the required information. It is tempting to include more information because you "really want the assessors to know" about your challenges, but you need to save that for another place, or omit it altogether. Keep it simple, stick to the instructions. For prompt 1, if you prefer, you can list the information instead of using paragraph form. This is the same information using another format that still fits within the allocated space:

Sample Response:

Grades 9–12 high school, multitrack, year-round, comprehensive, urban
5,200 students
Ethnicity: Hispanic—70%; African American—12%; Caucasian—9%; Native American—2%; Asian—3%; other—4%
Free and reduced lunch—80%
English Language Learners—74%
Departmentalized by subject
Average class size 30; ninth-grade English limited to 20 students per class, 100 per day

Gather the demographic information you need. Most schools now have this information on their websites. All schools must have this data available according to federal mandates. You may round off the percentages to whole numbers. Knowing this information also informs your teaching.

The second prompt is quite different from the first and allows for some choice about what to include or omit. It must be written in paragraph form. That there is a small amount of space indicates that the board is not seeking extensive explanations, just the facts as you see them. Remember that this is a snapshot. You will be going into detail about the class you feature when you write the Instructional Context at the beginning of each of the first three entries.

*Prompt 2. Write a **brief** paragraph containing information about your teaching context that **you believe would be important for assessors to know** [emphasis mine] in order to understand your portfolio entries. You might include details of any state or district mandates that may shape your teaching (including required curricula, standardized tests or other assessments, pacing, or texts). You might also include information regarding the type of community in which this teaching occurs, and the degree to which you have access to current technologies.*

Sample Response: I teach one self-contained, grades 1–2 combination class of 28 students of whom 4 have exceptional needs and are fully included. I have a classroom aide for 2 hours daily and a full-time aide for one of the students with exceptional needs. Our district mandates the use of a highly scripted reading program for 3 hours a day and a scripted math program for 2 hours daily. Students are tested every 4 weeks according to a district pacing plan and assessment tool, a challenge for students with exceptional needs, English Language Learners, and many other students. Our community of primarily first-generation working-class families trusts the public school and is supportive of our programs. I have 5 classroom computers, each with Internet access. Student turnover is 25% per year. Teacher turnover is nearly 50% annually.

In the second prompt I made choices about what to include although I was careful to address the prompt. I also didn't whine about the teaching situation, the mandates, the testing, or anything else—even if I might vehemently disagree with them or fully embrace them. This section is primarily objective. You have some choice about what to include in your response, but none of the choices include whining. The purpose of this section is to identify the big issues that shape your teaching context so the assessors can assess your teaching given your specific context. We want relevant information. It's relevant to my teaching if 25 percent of the students are transient during the year—units may be much shorter and getting to know my students may take longer and be a continual process. It's also relevant to how I work with colleagues if 50 percent of them are new to the school each year. Choose carefully because space is limited. Your response should reflect your teaching context.

Capture the Contextual Information Sheet from the Portable Document Format (PDF) file you have downloaded from the NB website, or from the CD-ROM you received with your box. Paste it into a text document so you can type directly into it. Or you can type a blank text document and cut, paste, and copy the completed work onto the sheet provided with your instructions. Use the specified font and do not exceed the allotted space. It's not fair to shrink the prompt text. Don't risk disqualification.

After you've written your first draft ask a colleague—preferably another candidate or NBCT—to read the prompts and check to see if you have responded to each part. Does the written work clearly communicate the information? If it does, you're done; if not, revise. Make four copies of your revised Contextual Information Sheet. Place one completed copy in each of the entry folders you now should have in your organization/collection box, and move on.

ENTRIES 1, 2, AND 3: PLANNING AHEAD

To fully understand the work that is required to complete the portfolio successfully, we're going to analyze each of the first three entries, extract the main ideas and what we have to do, and then record this information in the Portfolio Overview graphic organizer included at the end of this chapter. Having all of this information in one place will help you establish a time line and then adhere to it. It will also clarify the big picture for you, what you have to know and do during your candidacy. You can record your *completed* portfolio entries on the form included in the Resources section of your NB portfolio instructions.

INSTRUCTION FOR COMPLETING THE PORTFOLIO REVIEW

Entry Name and Summary

Return to the portfolio instructions for Entry 1. Read the overview on the first page. Highlight the key points. See if you can condense this entry into a single sentence. For example, after reading the MC Generalist Entry 1 *"Writing: Thinking through the Process,"* I could restate it as follows: *"Writing to learn and learning to write across the curriculum."* Of course, there's much more depth than I can capture in one sentence, but I know this entry is about writing, not just teaching kids how to write, but also using writing to acquire information and deepen their understanding. It also means I have to go beyond English Language Arts and incorporate writing in other disciplines as well. Enter your brief statement in the Portfolio Overview for Entry 1.

Standards Addressed

The standards addressed at the end of each overview are listed. Copy the number of the standards and the titles. Standards are frequently addressed in more than one entry. You will want to reread the standards before completing each entry and again after you have drafted your response before revising it.

The following information may be found in the directions for each entry on the page(s) titled "What Do I Need To Do?"

Evidence Required

Does the entry call for student work samples? What kind and how many? Is there a videotape requirement? How long and how many segments? Is this group work or whole class discussion or other? Be specific but brief.

Number of Students

In each entry you are either told exactly how many students to feature or you have some flexibility. For instance, if you have to do a whole-class video, the entry instructions do not say 30 students; you may have only 20, or you may have 40. In this column you would enter "Whole Class"; in another entry it might be "two small groups of 3–6 students each"; or two students' work samples. You may not feature the same students for multiple entries. However, if your certificate calls for a whole-group discussion, the students who appear in your whole-class video may also be in other entries.

Time Period Covered

Not all entries specify a time period, but nearly all track student progress over time. How much time? You want to know this now so you can plan ahead. Wouldn't it be a shame if you discovered in late February that to show adequate student progress you needed an 8-week period, but your portfolio is due at the end of March, which is only 6 weeks away? (This is a strong argument for student portfolios and collecting all students' work throughout the year.) Let's avoid surprises, overlapping, and missed directions. Carefully read the entry directions now so you'll know what you need to do and when.

Challenges?

How does this entry challenge me? This column requires self-analysis and reflection. What do you think you're going to find difficult? Will it be meeting the standards? Identifying which students to highlight? Videotaping? Conducting whole-group discussions that engage all students? Analyzing and writing about student progress? Once you've identified what you think might challenge you, you can prepare to strengthen those skills. For example, you might practice with the video camera, learn how to analyze student work to discover what they know not just what they've gotten wrong, and much more. Although it may feel intimidating to identify what you don't know, it's worse to complete the portfolio, submit it for assessment, and then fall short of certification because you hadn't strengthened the part(s) of your practice you could have improved.

REPEAT FOR ENTRY 2 AND ENTRY 3

At this point you have a good overall understanding of what you have to do to complete the portfolio entries. We examine Entry 4 separately because it is the only entry that is not based on student work.

CHECK FOR UNDERSTANDING

In the Resources section of your portfolio instructions return to the Summary of Portfolio Entries. Compare the information you've entered in your portfolio overview for Entries 1, 2, and 3 with the summary provided by the National Board. Later on, when you've analyzed Entry 4, you can save that information in your graphic organizer as well. Have you interpreted the entry requirements correctly? What have you misunderstood, if anything? Seek clarification if you are still not clear about what you need to do.

THE PORTFOLIO OVERVIEW—EXAMPLE

Certificate: ELA

	PORTFOLIO ENTRY 1	PORTFOLIO ENTRY 2	PORTFOLIO ENTRY 3	PORTFOLIO ENTRY 4
ENTRY NAME	**Analysis of Student Growth in Reading and Writing**	**Instructional Analysis: Whole Class Discussion**	**Instructional Analysis: Small Groups**	**Documented Accomplishments**
Standards Addressed	1, 2, 3, 6, 8, 9, 11, 13, and 14	1, 2, 3, 4, 5, 6, 7, 10, and 14	1, 2, 3, 4, 5, 6, 7, 10, and 14	14, 15, and 16
What Am I Asked to Do	• demonstrate how I teach students to read and write • describe goals for teaching • describe prompt that led to students response • describe my analysis of student's work • explain how these examples of student work collectively describe my instruction of reading and writing	• demonstrate my teaching strategies that I use for the whole class • to show my students and myself involved in a discussion about a topic, concept, or text important to my instruction	• demonstrate the teaching strategies that I use for small group discussion • show my facilitation and interaction with students • to interact with students intermittently as I circulate among the groups	• demonstrate my commitment to student learning through my work with families, community, learning, and collaborating • show what I do outside of the classroom that impacts what I do inside the classroom
Type of Evidence Required	• (13 pgs) Written Commentary on student work • Description • Analysis • Reflection	• (11 pgs) Written Commentary • Instructional Context (1 page) • Planning and Video Tape Analysis (6 pgs) • Reflection (4 pgs)	• (11 pgs) Written Commentary • Instructional Context (1 page) • Planning and Video Tape Analysis (6 pgs) • Reflection (4 pgs)	• Classroom Layout • Photo ID • (10 pgs) Description and Analysis of 8 accomplishments. • (16 pgs) Documentation

	PORTFOLIO ENTRY 1	PORTFOLIO ENTRY 2	PORTFOLIO ENTRY 3	PORTFOLIO ENTRY 4
ENTRY NAME	**Analysis of Student Growth in Reading and Writing**	**Instructional Analysis: Whole Class Discussion**	**Instructional Analysis: Small Groups**	**Documented Accomplishments**
Type of Evidence Required (continued)	• Student A packet with 4 responses • Student B packet with 4 responses • (15 min) Videotape	• Submitted Instructional Materials (3 pgs) • Classroom Layout • Photo ID	• (15 min) Videotape • Submitted Instructional Materials	• (2 pgs) Reflective Summary
Number of Kids	2 students	Whole Class	Whole Class/small groups	N/A
Time Period Covered in This Entry	One unit	Before the videotape segment, the video tape, and the analysis after the tape in context of the whole year	Before the videotape segment, the video tape, and the analysis after the tape in context of the whole year	For documentation of parent/community = this year As a learner = last 5 years As a collaborator = last 5 years
How Does This Entry Challenge Me?	Analyzing a reading assignment my students complete, and use what I learn from the students in my teaching	Integrating reading, writing, listening, speaking, viewing and producing media texts at the same time	Establishing small groups and videotaping them effectively	I feel that I haven't accomplished much, because it is hard for me to see myself in this light

THE PORTFOLIO OVERVIEW WORKSHEET

Certificate:

ENTRY NAME	PORTFOLIO ENTRY 1 Analysis of Student Growth in Reading and Writing	PORTFOLIO ENTRY 2 Instructional Analysis: Whole Class Discussion	PORTFOLIO ENTRY 3 Instructional Analysis: Small Groups	PORTFOLIO ENTRY 4 Documented Accomplishments
Standards Addressed				
What Am I Asked To Do				
Type of Evidence Required				
# of Kids				
Time Period Covered in This Entry				
How Does This Entry Challenge Me?				

8 KNOWLEDGE OF STUDENTS

There's no doubt that the National Board deliberately chose to begin with the core proposition *Teachers Are Committed to Students and Their Learning*. Every certificate has one or more standards that refer to knowing our students. Just how committed are you? I know you show up for school every day, you try your best, but because we teach based upon what we believe, it's important that we identify our core beliefs. If you've studied the *Teacher's Guide*, you have already been thinking about your core beliefs. However, they are worth reflecting on again because our ideas and beliefs change over time. The following reflections will help you to examine your core beliefs:

1. Using your reflective journal, quickly list 10 adjectives, words, or phrases you would use to describe your students. Don't do any editing yet, just list the ideas as they come to you.

2. Read your list. Imagine someone else is reading it, someone who doesn't know you. What would they say you believe about your students? Now, what does your list tell you about your beliefs? About your perception of your students' ability to learn? About your role as their teacher?

3. Here are the big questions: How do your beliefs about your students impact your teaching? Your students' learning?

Let's return to the NB standards. Reread the standard(s) for your certificate that most closely reflects knowledge of students (Knowledge of Students, Equity, Fairness, and Diversity, other). Examine the personal inventory chart(s) you've already completed. How do your current beliefs about your students match the National Board's core propositions? The NB standards? How do they vary? Why is this important?

Remember that your writing must be concrete, not abstract. Provide concrete examples from your current practice that demonstrate what you believe about your students and their learning. These are the actions, strategies, choices you make for them. What would your practice look like if you were completely committed to students and their learning as defined in the NB standards? Again, think of concrete examples. You may have already written some in your inventory charts.

In the portfolio instructions you'll be asked to identify one or more students and then, using the students' learning as examples, describe your teaching. Let's get ready by reflecting on two or more current students or ones from the recent past. (Challenging students are actually easier to write about and to impact than are highly gifted, self-motivated students. You'll find a section on Making Good Choices in the instructions for each portfolio entry.)

As you identify the instructional goals and strategies to assist students in reaching those goals, it's important that your choices demonstrate that you know your students, understand their interests and needs, and relate to how they learn. Instructional planning is influenced by what we know about our students. Here are some things to consider that students carry with them when they enter your classroom for the first time:

THE THINGS THEY CARRY

Age	Gender	Personal perspectives
Appearance	Goals	Preferences
Assumptions	History	Prior Knowledge
Communication style	Hormones	Religion
Culture	Impulses	Socio-economic status
Education	Misconceptions	Values and Beliefs
Emotions	Opinions	Wants and Needs
Experiences		

Although no one expects you to know everything about every student, especially if you teach more than one class each day, you can know some things about each student. What is most important for your portfolio entry is that when you have knowledge about a student, you address it. More about this when we explore the Instructional Context (Chapter 9) included with your entries.

Reflection

How does (did) your teaching of these students reflect the NB standards? Why does this matter?

9 INSTRUCTIONAL CONTEXT

The written commentary for each of the first three entries begins with the "Instructional Context," suggested length one page (two pages on a few certificates). This differs from the Contextual Information. Contextual Information is a snapshot of your school/district. The Instructional Context, on the other hand, is a more in-depth view of your class—the one you feature in each entry. You are instructed to describe and analyze the instructional context—those factors, especially the factors related to the students, that influence the teaching choices. You may feature a different class for each of the three entries or use the same one. You may also choose to use the same class, but highlight different *relevant* characteristics of the class for each entry. The choice is yours.

As with the rest of the NB process, gathering and analyzing information about your current class(es) of students, although important for the assessors, is even more important for you. Who is in your class(es)? What do they know? What can they already do? What misconceptions do they have, if any? What special interests do they share? Who are the students with exceptional needs and what are those needs? (Consult Chapter 8, "Knowledge of Students." Reread the NB standard Knowledge of Students.) We should make instructional choices based upon who is in our class(es).

Each class in each of my 12 years in the classroom presented different challenges: students' needs changed, their ability levels fluctuated, the community's expectations increased. And each year my own knowledge level and range of available strategies grew. Just as I had different students each year, I was also different each year I entered the classroom. I was reading a different variety of books and had had more professional experiences. And the world around us had changed and continued to change. All of this impacted my instructional choices. Accomplished teachers don't deliver *canned* lessons devoid of consideration of students' needs and abilities or lessons free from consideration of the teaching context. We must always be cognizant that we teach students first, then curriculum.

The portfolio instructions prompt you about what to include in each part of your written commentary. These prompts are your writing guide. I recommend that you set up your pages in advance by formatting according to the NB guidelines (1-inch margins, 12 point Times New Roman font, double spaced). Put your candidate number in the upper-right header and the page and entry number in the lower-right footer of each page. For your drafts, type the prompts directly onto this page in bold italics (or cut and paste from the electronic portfolio instructions). As you proceed to write your commentary, answer each prompt exactly, even when the prompts appear redundant. Later, when you are revising and remove the prompts (you don't want to waste the limited page space on prompts), you'll find that you have a well-written commentary. Try to stay within the one or two page suggested allowance. Writing more in this section means you'll have less room for commentary in the following sections.

You may begin each section immediately following the prior section, without beginning a new page. You want to use all of the pages allowed for your commentary and not waste space just to make the entry pretty. Use a heading identifying each new section as follows:

Instructional Context:

XXXXXXXXXXXXXXXXXXXXXXXXXXXXXXXXXXXXXXXXXXXXXX.

    Xxxxxxxxxxxxxxxxxxxxxxxxxxxxxxxxxxxxxxxxxxxxxxxxxxxxx xxxxxxxxxxx.

    Xxxxxxxxxxxxxxxxxxxxxxxxxxxxxxxxxxxxxxxxxxxxxxxxxxxxx xxxxxx.

Planning and Teaching Analysis:

XXXXXXXXXXXXXXXXXXXXXXXXXXXXXXX.

WRITING THE INSTRUCTIONAL CONTEXT

The first two prompts require fairly objective responses, but the third and fourth prompts in this section are more subjective and reflect your knowledge of your students and of your class and school environment. We began this workbook by examining our beliefs about students; here's where your beliefs become transparent. All of the certificates have basically the same prompts; you should respond to the exact prompts included in your portfolio instructions. Sample responses are included following each prompt.

Prompt. What is your school setting (e.g. preschool, middle, or high school, alternative school)? What are the number, ages, and grades of the students featured in this entry and subject matter of the class?

Sample Response: I teach in a comprehensive high school. In this regular English Language Arts class there are 32 students, ages 14–16; 28 are 9th graders, 3 are 10th graders repeating the class.

Prompt. What are the relevant characteristics of this class that influenced your instructional strategies for this theme or topic of concern: ethnic, cultural, and linguistic diversity; the range of abilities of the students; the personality of the class?

Sample Response: This class is more diverse than the student body at large. There are 12 Hispanic students, 11 Asians, 7 African Americans, and 2 Caucasians; 17 boys, 15 girls. There is a wide range of abilities, especially in writing skills and style; some write complete essays; others are working on paragraphs. The majority of the students are subdued, but because I enjoy a verbally active class and like to promote considerable academic discourse, they've been getting more vocal and more engaged with one another throughout the semester. All of the students speak English, although the conventions of standard English are a struggle.

Prompt. What are the relevant features of your teaching context that influenced the selection of this theme or topic? This might include other realities of the social and physical teaching context (e.g., available resources, scheduling of classes, self-contained classroom, etc.) that are relevant to your response.

Sample Response: Our department divides students into remedial, regular, honors, and advanced classes. I choose to teach remedial and regular classes and I hold high expectations for all students and teach accordingly. Although we have state-mandated standards, they are general enough to allow me to select themes that are relevant for my students. We use our five classroom computers and Internet access to obtain lots of the texts we use in class. Our desks are constantly reconfigured to meet our needs, groups, lecture style, debate teams, etc.

Prompt. What particular instructional challenges do the students chosen for this entry represent? Explain the particular dynamics of the class an assessor needs to know to understand how you involve students in establishing a supporting and stimulating community and how you used your topic of discussion to assist students in accomplishing this goal. This *might include, but is not limited to, a description of your students' skills, knowledge, and previous experiences that relate to your teaching.*

Sample Response: During this election year, democracy has been a central theme, and reading, analyzing, and debating political speeches has been the focus of the curriculum for this unit. These students are used to completing worksheets and being quiet, not having and sharing their own ideas. A challenge has been to open their minds and encourage their voices. To prepare students to participate in our democracy, they need to have democracy in their lives. I do a lot of scaffolding, break the text into readable chunks, jigsaw, preread, hold Socratic seminars, and use many other strategies to reduce the barriers to understanding. The cultural differences break down over time as students gain personal voice.

The NB prompt uses the word *relevant*. You can't possibly write everything about your class and students in one page. The prompts are guides assisting you as you make choices about what information to provide in the limited available space. As you make those choices, consider what is *relevant*. There's lots going on, shortened schedules on some days, PA announcements on others, but not all of it is relevant to this entry. A feature is relevant, and should be included in your descriptions, if it impacts your teaching choices. For example, if students have different cultural backgrounds and you include multicultural materials in your instructional choices, you would include that feature in your description.

Caution: I have read entries wherein candidates displayed a thorough knowledge of their students, their cultural backgrounds, interests, skill levels, special needs, and challenges for teaching. These candidates did an excellent job of setting the stage for the assessor to understand the candidate's teaching context. But it is insufficient to know the characteristics of your teaching context if you don't put that knowledge to good use. When the candidate connects the relevant characteristics of the teaching context to the instructional choices, evidence of student achievement usually follows. But if a candidate describes students' needs and then ignores those needs when making instructional choices, we don't find evidence of accomplished teaching. In fact, if after writing a description of the Contextual Information and the Instructional Context, you discover that you have not addressed some of the identified students' needs in your analysis of the featured lesson and the student work, you might consider omitting some of the characteristics you mentioned, or revising your commentary to include how you responded to students' needs, or reteaching and selecting a different unit to feature that shows your work as an accomplished teacher—sensitive and responsive to students.

Failure to use the information about your school setting and/or students to impact instructional decisions is worse than not knowing about your students at all. An accomplished teacher does not intentionally ignore an identified student need or strength. Accomplished teachers use their knowledge about students to make instructional choices and to provide differentiated instruction. If you are going to describe Contextual Features and Instructional Context, it is important to specifically reference, in the body of your entry, how your instruction and choice of strategies addressed identified student characteristics.

Draft the Contextual Information and Instructional Context sheet and ask other educators, preferably candidates, to read and comment on them. How to comment on one another's work is included in a chapter on Cohort Groups (Chapter 16). Remember, the purpose of these two sections, "Contextual Information" and "Instructional Context," is to set the stage so the assessors examine your teaching practice as it relates to your teaching context, not to an idealized version of what school should look like, but as your teaching reflects where and who you teach.

PLANNING AND INSTRUCTION

Each of the first three portfolio entries asks you to analyze your planning and teaching (not in these exact words): *What instructional goals do you have for your students? Why are these worthwhile goals for these students at this time? How do these goals fit into your overall yearlong goals? What strategies did you use to help students meet these goals?*

In this section of the portfolio entry, begin with your long-term goals and work toward the specific goals for the featured lesson(s).

For example: *Democracy is one of my long-term goals. I want students, many of whom are first-generation Americans, to be actively engaged citizens who participate by understanding the democratic system as practiced in the United States, voting, calling upon their elected officials, and contributing to society. In the featured unit, we are reading and analyzing political speeches. We are learning to extract factual information from subjective comments designed to persuade us through our emotions so that we can make informed choices. We read and annotate text, conduct Socratic seminars, analyze word choices, write persuasive speeches, and participate in debates. We write formal letters and e-mail memos to our elected officials expressing our opinions and requesting they address our concerns. We conduct the class as a model of democracy, including choice, responsibility and accountability, and pay attention to what is best for the class citizens—the students and teacher—and open our classroom to parents and other community members.*

The prompts in this section move you from overarching goals to specific goals and strategies for the student work featured in the entry. The goals should be important and relevant, worthy of your students' time and attention, and presented in a manner that reflects their importance in and beyond the academic environment. The overarching instructional goals you feature in your portfolio entries should lead students to essential understanding about the world around them.

11 TEACHING STRATEGIES

The strategies you select to help students achieve the goals should be varied and empowering. Patrick Finn, building upon the work of Brazilian educator Paolo Friere, identifies strategies that provide a liberating education and lead to student independence. Check your own practice to see if the strategies you regularly employ lead to student independence, a major feature of accomplished teachers' classrooms. Here are some examples of empowering strategies. Although you probably don't rely on these strategies exclusively, they should form an important part of your teaching tool box:

- ☐ Knowledge is rarely presented as facts isolated from wider bodies of knowledge.
- ☐ Knowledge taught is related to students' lives and experiences.
- ☐ Work is challenging.
- ☐ Creativity, analysis, and expression are honored.
- ☐ Discussion of challenges to the status quo, past and present, frequently occurs.
- ☐ Instruction is rarely copying notes, filling in the blanks, or multiple choice.
- ☐ Students are given choices and rewarded for original solutions.
- ☐ We learn to write and write to deepen understanding.
- ☐ Textbook knowledge is validated and challenged by analyzing multiple texts.
- ☐ Art work may supplement the writing process.
- ☐ Students have considerable freedom of movement and access to materials.
- ☐ Students are rewarded for initiative and inquisitiveness.
- ☐ The teacher focuses on expression and content before correctness.

Whenever possible, go public with your teaching by expanding the audience for student work, inviting collaboration with students outside your class and with parents and colleagues, using public texts as well as academic ones (newspaper, television, Internet, nonfiction works, textbooks, nonprint texts such as film and art objects).

As a mentor teacher for nine years and in my professional development consulting I've observed in many classrooms and viewed hundreds of video-taped entries. Some classroom practices are dynamic—students are engaged in meaningful ways—whereas other classrooms lack energy. There is also a marked difference between students simply participating in an activity and students truly engaged in learning. Assessors are not looking for lots of activities—activities are time-fillers and time-wasters—they are looking for empowering strategies that move students toward achieving the instructional goals. The level and content of classroom discourse, which is evident in your videotaped entries, are the distinguishing features of empowering education. You can improve the level of your classroom discourse, a key feature of every videotape, by teaching students how to ask questions at every level.

Transcribing one of your videos will give you a true picture of the discourse activity in your class and the types of questions you ask. To enhance the quality of your classroom discourse, engage students in asking and answering questions at multiple levels. Level 3 questions, as described in the following list, are by far the most interesting. Questions should be not only from teacher to student but between students, and from students to teacher.

- [ ] Level 1 questions. These questions can be answered explicitly by facts contained in the text or by information accessible in other resources. Answers are frequently short, seldom more than a word or phrase.
- [ ] Level 2 questions. The answers to these questions are implied in the text. They require analysis and interpretation of specific parts of the text.
- [ ] Level 3 questions. These questions are more open-ended and go beyond the text. They are intended to provoke a discussion of an abstract idea or issue. These questions often attempt to connect the text, or an idea within the text, to another discipline.

Accomplished teachers command a wide range of teaching strategies and know how and when to use them. I've included a check sheet of proven effective strategies at the end of this chapter. It is not an exhaustive list of teaching strategies. You may know many of these practices by other names. If you find that you don't have a wide range of strategies in your teacher's tool box, you might want to search out information, workshops, and colleagues who know and effectively use strategies you are not currently familiar with. Seek professional development opportunities that will enrich your practice. I know that there is no single set of strategies effective with all students. Therefore, it is critically important that we come to the classroom prepared with multiple strategies so we can address the needs of each of our students in the most effective ways possible.

After you've reviewed the Effective Teaching Strategies, take the time to do the reflection on page 58. Remember, accomplished teachers are mindful; they think about their practice and learn from their experiences.

EFFECTIVE TEACHING:
STRATEGIES IDENTIFIED WITH STUDENT GAINS

Effective teachers regularly use a variety of strategies. Depending upon the instructional goal, effective teachers select specific strategies to help students achieve the goals. The list of strategies that follows is not meant to be exhaustive. It does, however, include those strategies shown to be most effective in aiding student learning. *The NB portfolio instructions ask you to identify your instructional goals and the strategies you use to assist students in achieving those goals.*

For each of the following strategies circle the number indicating how often you use the strategy according to the following scale:

1	Never
2	Seldom
3	Sometimes
4	Frequently
5	Very Frequently

STRATEGY*	SCALE				
Begin a lesson with a short review of previous learning, connect to future lessons/units, make interdisciplinary connections.	1	2	3	4	5
Begin a lesson with a short statement of instructional goals.	1	2	3	4	5
Make connections to the standard(s).	1	2	3	4	5
Give clear and detailed instructions and explanations.	1	2	3	4	5
Ask a large number of questions, check for student understanding, and obtain responses from all students.	1	2	3	4	5
Present new material in small steps, providing for student practice after each step.	1	2	3	4	5
Provide for high-level student practice.	1	2	3	4	5
Guide students during initial practice.	1	2	3	4	5
Monitor students during seatwork.	1	2	3	4	5
Check for student misconceptions and correct those misconceptions.	1	2	3	4	5
Provide feedback in a timely manner (48 hours or less for graded work) from teacher, other students, on computers.	1	2	3	4	5

Note: These strategies are loosely adapted from "Teaching Functions," by B. Rosenshine and R. Stevens, 1986, in M. C. Wittrock (Ed.). *Handbook of Research on Teaching* (pp. 376–391). Additions drawn from teaching experiences. (See http://epaa.asu.edu/barak/barak/html.)

STRATEGY	SCALE				
Teach students to generate questions at all levels.	1	2	3	4	5
Employ think-aloud strategies as a model/scaffold for students.	1	2	3	4	5
Allow time for student thinking about their thinking and learning (metacognition).	1	2	3	4	5
Reflect on your teaching effectiveness.	1	2	3	4	5
Scaffold tasks through modeling and/or cue cards or checklists until students achieve mastery.	1	2	3	4	5
Provide procedural prompts, such as sentence starters. (How are ___ and ___ alike? What is the main idea of _____?)	1	2	3	4	5
Provide models of sample responses.	1	2	3	4	5
Anticipate and discuss potential difficulties.	1	2	3	4	5
Regulate the difficulty of the task.	1	2	3	4	5
Provide and teach a checklist or scoring guide (rubric).	1	2	3	4	5
Provide independent practice with new examples.	1	2	3	4	5
Increase student responsibilities (Never do what a student can—and should—do).	1	2	3	4	5
Help students organize new material (graphic organizers, mind mapping).	1	2	3	4	5
Use standards based student portfolios with time for student analysis, reflection, and self-assessment.	1	2	3	4	5
Examine student work to improve your teaching effectiveness.	1	2	3	4	5

Reflection

Select one of the effective teaching strategies listed on pages 56–57 for which you rated yourself a 4 or 5. Briefly describe what that strategy looks like in your classroom practice. Give a specific example. Think of when you use the strategy, under what conditions, for what instructional goals, why this strategy is the best choice for your students and the lesson. Show, don't tell.

12 VIDEOTAPING

Depending upon the certificate, two or three of your portfolio entries require videotaping. The specific requirements for each entry are outlined in the portfolio instructions. Follow the instructions exactly.

The "Get Started" section of the instructions contains Tips for Videotaping. The National Board has done an excellent job of gathering information and instructions for videotaping your entries. Included are suggested equipment and graphics layouts for best camera placement. I'm not going to duplicate the information you can easily access through your portfolio instructions; I'm going to supplement it.

☐ Camera person. I strongly suggest that you do not use a professional videographer, or even a local college student interested in film. I've learned from experience that videographers and film students want to be directors, wanting to show off their craft. Using one of your students presents another challenge; that a given student may want to film his or her friends more than the others. Young students bounce around everywhere and try to follow the speaker instead of holding the camera in one position or moving from group to group as directed.

 • Other teachers working toward certification or parents you recruit to assist you tend to make the best camera persons. A viable alternative is the audio/visual (AV) person at school or an administrator you recruit for the purpose. This video is not about creating a movie, it's about your teaching.

 • Video as a teaching strategy. Until I worked toward certification I had not used the video camera as a teaching tool, but it is an excellent tool. Videotape student presentations, videotape group work, videotape Socratic seminars (an excellent way to hold a whole-class discussion) and then show and discuss the video with your students. Ask them to help you analyze the tape. Ask specific students what they were doing when their head was down or their hand was waving or when they were seemingly staring into space. I learn a great deal from my students' analysis, and so do they.

- Use the video to supplement student portfolios during student-led conferences. Students love to show their performances to their families and friends.
- You can purchase an older-model video camera, preferably a VHS model, very inexpensively through an online auction. The bigger the camera, the better it is for classroom use and the less expensive to purchase. You can set it on a tripod and no one will want to walk away with it.

☐ Quality verbal interaction. Some classroom practices are dynamic, where students are engaged in meaningful ways; other classrooms lack energy. There is also a marked difference between students engaged in an activity (i.e., throwing paper balls into a basket when they spell a word correctly) and really focused on learning. Assessors are not looking for lots of activity; they are looking for quality engagement.

- Patrick Finn, author of *Literacy with an Attitude*, identifies the level and content of classroom discourse as one of the distinguishing features between domesticating and liberating or empowering education. You can improve the level of your classroom discourse, a key feature of every videotape, by teaching students how to ask questions at every level. Students shouldn't be responding only to the teacher's questions, but to questions posed by other students as well.
- Did you know?
  - 85 percent of classroom conversation consists of the teacher asking questions of the students.
  - 85 percent of those questions are known-response questions. (The teacher already knows the answer and the student knows the teacher knows.) Students sometimes refer to this kind of questioning as "guessing what's on the teacher's mind."
  - Teachers usually wait an average of less than 3 seconds between the time they ask a student a question and the time they expect an answer. Learn to wait up to 3 minutes. Waiting provides a more equal opportunity to respond and learn for students who are more thoughtful than they are quick.

☐ Transcription. Transcribing one of your videos will give you a true picture of the discourse activity in your class. Take the time to transcribe portions of your tapes, especially the one you decide to submit with your portfolio. You can insert the quotes you gather through transcription into your analysis commentary and thus highlight important points for the assessors.

☐ Three-level questions. To enhance the quality of your classroom discourse, encourage students to ask and answer questions at multiple levels. Level-3 questions, as defined in Chapter 11, are by far the most interesting. Questions should be not only from teacher to student, but between students and from students to teacher. It is often more difficult to frame a question than it is to answer one. Thus, asking questions may be the more accurate assessment of a student's understanding than answering a level-1 question would be.

☐ Analyze. The analysis questions supplied with the portfolio instructions are an excellent reflective tool. I've also included a video analysis questionnaire, another lens through which to view your video. Don't expect to score a 5 in every category; the video analysis questionnaire is intended as a guide and check sheet.

VIDEOTAPE ANALYSIS GUIDE

For each of the following strategies, circle the number indicating how often you use the strategy according to the following scale:

1	Not at All
2	Infrequently or Slightly
3	Sometimes or Somewhat
4	Often
5	Continually or Highly

For each of the following questions, circle the number to the right that best fits your objective observation of the videotape using the preceding scale. You may have to stretch your response to the question to have the answer fit. Keep your mind on the purpose and don't get lost in the minutia. Some of the questions may overlap. The purpose is to enable you to get an overall sense of your teaching or of your colleague's teaching. (These questions have been loosely adapted from the NBPTS Instructions.)

OBSERVATION		SCALE			
1. Students talking/asking questions.	1	2	3	4	5
2. Student engagement (body language, facial expressions)	1	2	3	4	5
3. Teacher to students—Level-1 questions	1	2	3	4	5
4. Teacher to students—Level-2 questions	1	2	3	4	5
5. Teacher to students—Level-3 questions	1	2	3	4	5

(table continues on next page)

6. Students to teacher—Level-1 questions	1	2	3	4	5
7. Students to teacher—Level-2 questions	1	2	3	4	5
8. Students to teacher—Level-3 questions	1	2	3	4	5
9. Students' overall interaction with teacher	1	2	3	4	5
10. Students' interactions with one another	1	2	3	4	5
11. Making connections to students' prior knowledge	1	2	3	4	5
12. Connecting to future learning	1	2	3	4	5
13. Making connections to information/experiences beyond the classroom	1	2	3	4	5
14. Students taking intellectual risks	1	2	3	4	5
15. Put-downs by teacher/other students	1	2	3	4	5
16. Establishing clear learning goals/outcomes	1	2	3	4	5
17. Responding to student misconceptions	1	2	3	4	5
18. Taking advantage of unexpected teachable moments	1	2	3	4	5
19. Differentiated instructional opportunities	1	2	3	4	5
20. Accommodations, if appropriate, for ELD students	1	2	3	4	5
21. Accommodations, if appropriate, for students with special needs	1	2	3	4	5

Reflection

A strength I observed . . .

An area needing improvement . . .

Suggested ways to improve . . .

I (the teacher) will know I've (he/she) improved when . . .

13 ANALYZING STUDENT WORK

In the National Board context, although you are analyzing student work, the assessors are not interested in the individual featured students per se. They are using the students, what you write about them and their work, and the samples you provide *to learn about your teaching*. This is a very important distinction. Select students for whom you have made a substantial difference, students you have helped and empowered through your teaching.

The portfolio entries require that you include samples of student work as evidence of effective teaching. The merit of any teaching technique is judged by its ability to improve the intellectual quality of student performance. The work you assign must be worthy of students' time and effort. The student's work should show improvement as a result of your teaching. Refrain from putting any negative or sarcastic or unhelpful remarks on students' papers. The feedback you provide should move students forward in intellectual quality or skill ability.

You will know and be able to explain that you've added value to students when you identify what they knew and could do at point A and what they know and can do at points B, C, and maybe even D. Along the way you analyze students' progress and make teaching decisions based on what you learn by analyzing students' work.

A RUBRIC IS A GUIDE

In each entry, carefully read and think about the criteria for measurement as explained in the level-4 rubric included with the portfolio instructions. Highlight the active verbs and use them in your response. Demonstrate through explicit references to your actions, to the actions of other students, and to the featured student work that you have successfully incorporated each of the teaching ideas listed in the rubric. After you've written your first draft, return to the rubric to verify that you have indeed met each of these criteria and have adequately explained yourself in the written response. You will not have the benefit of speaking with the assessors and supplementing orally what you omitted to put in writing; your written response stands alone!

LOOKING AT STUDENT WORK TO IMPROVE INSTRUCTION

We are more used to grading student work than analyzing it. We grade the student paper, return it, and move on. Looking at student work to improve instruction, as well as to advance students' learning, is very different and more rewarding. In your analysis of the student work begin by noting which skills/competencies the student has achieved. Then continue your analysis by stating what the student needs, or needed, to do to attain the instructional goals. The assessment and the student work you've selected to feature should align with your stated instructional goals and therefore be an appropriate instrument for measuring student progress. Consider the challenges the student poses and plan accordingly. One size, one instructional technique definitely does not fit all. There is an expectation that you are tailoring, to some extent, instruction based on the student's needs.

In the "Get Started" section of the portfolio instructions are some Practice Activities. The guiding questions contained on these pages are helpful in pushing you to think about your students' work, not just grade it.

SAY. MEAN. MATTER.

Here's a technique that will help you understand and answer the prompts. When you read the prompt for each section, ask yourself what the prompt is saying, what it means, why it matters, and why the assessors want to know this bit of information. Use the following examples to practice analyzing the prompts. The more you understand the underlying reasoning behind each of the prompts, the more likely you will make good choices and explain your teaching practices *clearly, consistently,* and *convincingly.*

Sample Prompt 1. Who is the student you have chosen? Describe the kind of challenge the student represents.

Say. The assessor wants background information about the student and why you chose to feature this student.

Mean. This means that I should choose the student carefully, someone I know as an individual and respond to accordingly. The rubric states *recognize students' individual learning differences.*

Matter. The challenge is to teach the individual student in the context of a group. What differentiation, if needed, have I provided?

Sample Prompt 2. How was the student's responsibility for his or her own learning and development [as a writer] encouraged through these activities?

Say. How did the student monitor and manage his or her own learning? What strategies do I use to foster personal responsibility for learning?

Mean. It's not enough that the teacher monitors students' learning, students must also know the instructional goals and periodically assess their own progress. Teaching must incorporate strategies and time for students to monitor their own learning.

Matter. This is important because students who learn to manage their own learning acquire a skill with lifetime merit. Accomplished teachers recognize the importance and take the time to teach this skill.

Sample Prompt 3. Identify critical moments or choices made during instruction that impacted the direction of the lessons.

Say. The prompt is about choices before and during teaching.

Mean. It means that we don't learn by doing, we learn by thinking about what we're doing. It means we have to be cognizant of those teachable moments and not so bound to the plan that we refuse to alter course when the occasion suggests it.

Matter. This is difficult in my context because our school mandate requires I use a scripted reading program. How do I both pay attention to students' needs and follow the mandates? *Or* Accomplished teachers plan ahead but remain flexible to the students' needs.

BE SPECIFIC WHEN ANALYZING STUDENT WORK

You do not demonstrate knowledge of student, curriculum, or effective strategies when you write *Student A can't read*. The assessors know you are accomplished when you can identify the reading difficulty, for example, through specific analysis. *Student A can't read* may mean *Student A cannot predict what will occur next* or *Student A reads slowly and ignores punctuation*. When you identify the student's needs with some specificity, you can, and should, direct instruction accordingly. You also demonstrate that you know how to teach the subject so students can learn—one of the core propositions.

PRACTICE

Examine a piece of student work, one you might consider using as portfolio evidence. What does the student know how to do? What is missing from the student's work? Focus on quality over quantity. What do you need to do to help the student to achieve? What did you do? Did it work? Why or why not? The more you think about your teaching, the more effective the teaching and the greater the student learning.

ENTRY 4: DOCUMENTED ACCOMPLISHMENTS

Entry 4, Documented Accomplishments, is about the work you do beyond your traditional classroom practice *that impacts student learning.* There is little variation between certificates for this entry, so I'll deal with all of the certificates at one time. In the other entries, you use student work samples as evidence supporting your analysis; this entry requires evidence from outside your classroom. Multiple examples of documents accepted as evidence are clearly explained in the portfolio instructions.

There are three categories addressed in the Documented Accomplishments entry:

1. *Your life as a learner over the past 4 years plus the current year of candidacy.* What have you done to consciously and deliberately continue your professional growth? These accomplishments may be through formal coursework or workshops or informal activities such as reading a professional book. The key words are *consciously* and *deliberately.*

2. *Your work as a leader and professional collaborator over the past 4 years plus the current year of candidacy.* This section refers to those activities you engage in with your colleagues and your contributions to the profession. Again, these can be formal connections, as in mentoring or supervising a student teacher, or less formal professional learning networks. Your contributions can be directed to your site colleagues or to the wider education community. Your focus is on improving teaching and learning, not just fulfilling a teacher's basic responsibilities.

3. *Activities to engage your students' families and the community in students' learning during the year in which you are working toward board certification.* Documented accomplishments in this area are those appropriate activities that go beyond what is expected. Meeting with parents at an open house is usually part of a teacher's responsibility. Documented accomplishment activities go beyond the requirements of the teacher's job; they are interactive, not one-way. The emphasis here is on actively engaging families and communities as teaching and learning partners.

Some of the accomplishments will overlap two or three categories. That's fine. Originally these accomplishments were divided into two portfolio entries. When the board realized how many activities were overlapping, it combined them into one entry. You still must show accomplishment in each category, but each accomplishment doesn't have to be unique to one category only. Neither do you need to have an equal number of accomplishments for each of the three categories. For instance, if you teach a professional course, you are both a professional collaborator, you contribute to your profession, and you're continuing your own learning—the best way to reinforce learning is to teach. If you have the Junior Achievement program in your class, for example, you are engaging volunteers from the business community as teachers of your students. If some of your families work as volunteers with the Junior Achievement program or some other structured program, you are learning while working collaboratively within the community and engaging family members as valued teaching and learning partners.

Your task is to describe the accomplishment, analyze its significance, and report its impact on student learning. The assessors are trained to find evidence of the applicable standards wherever they occur in the entry, and that includes within your written analysis, in the concluding reflection, and in the pages of documentation you supply.

Every accomplishment you describe in this entry must be connected to student learning. Therefore, you won't list committee meetings you may have participated in but that went nowhere. If you read professional journals but can't think of how you related what you read to your classroom practice and to student learning, it's not an accomplishment to be documented in this entry. Staff development workshops you were mandated to attend but that didn't improve your teaching also don't belong in these pages. Likewise, having parents bake cakes for fund-raisers or attend Open House is insufficient to demonstrate you engage parents or community members as active teaching and learning partners. Whichever activities you choose to describe for this entry, you must show a connection between the accomplishment and student learning. The students can be in your classes or in the classes of other teachers. The impact can be local, site-specific, or far-reaching.

You are limited to a maximum of eight accomplishments, so choose carefully.

Instructions

1. Read the italicized overview on the first pages of Entry 4 in your certificate's portfolio instructions. Highlight the key ideas, the active verbs. By doing a close read, you'll get some ideas for activities while you're also reminded of activities in which you've engaged in the past but might not have considered.

2. Reread the standards that are addressed in this entry. After each entry overview, the specific standards to address are listed. Entry 4 usually has three standards. Of course, because all of the standards are based on the five core propositions, and because the five core propositions are interrelated, no standard exists in isolation.

3. Enter your accomplishments in the graphic organizer included at the end of this chapter. (Duplicate page as needed.) The purpose here is to make certain that you highlight accomplishments in each of the three categories.

4. Talk to other teachers. If you have a cohort group, meet with it to discuss Entry 4. Ask what activities other teachers have done that fit into any of the three designated categories. From this informal survey, enter those activities that you've accomplished but perhaps hadn't thought of until mentioned by another teacher. Note those activities that you may want to incorporate in the future.

5. Before you write up an activity of your own, we'll examine an activity from another portfolio. Then you'll select one accomplishment you have already completed, describe it, include why the activity is significant in your teaching context, and state the impact on student learning.

Note: All of the entries in the portfolio require the same type of writing: description, analysis, and reflection. What did you do? What does it mean? Why does this activity matter to students? Ultimately, how does this accomplishment or series of accomplishments represent you as an accomplished teacher?

☐ *Description.* What did you do? (Activity/What?)

☐ *Analysis.* What does this mean? (Significance/So What?)

☐ *Analysis and Reflection.* Why does this matter? (Impact on student learning/Then what?)

Examining an Activity for Entry 4

Instructions

1. In pairs or triads read through the example accomplishment that follows the instructions.
2. Summarize what the candidate's entry Says.
3. What does this accomplishment Mean to the participants?
4. Discuss how the accomplishment addresses the standards.

Example: Title of Accomplishment: Student-Led Conferences

Description: What Is the Nature of This Accomplishment?

Every 10 weeks, four times each school year, to coincide with our report cards, I conduct student-led conferences. I first learned about student-led conferences at an English teachers' conference and subsequently read two books on the topic that outlined the theory and the mechanics of putting student-led conferences together. The conferences are in the evening to accommodate my students' families, most of whom are unable to attend day-time meetings and who would otherwise be left out of our school community. I was the first teacher at my school to hold student-led conferences in addition to the required semiannual open house meetings. Evening meetings are conducted on unpaid time but are very worthwhile nevertheless. Because many of my students live in foster care settings, all adults who play a significant role in the child's life are invited to attend, and do. Students have an opportunity, uninterrupted by me, to explain what they are doing in school and to discuss the progress they are making toward meeting the mandated standards. The students use their portfolios, a collection of the work they have done in class, and the mandated district standards as the focus of their conference.

Analysis and Reflection: Why Is This Accomplishment Significant?

These conferences are very significant to my students and to their families. Sometimes they are the only time students and families have meaningful conversation about schoolwork, or students are able to ask for assistance and be proud of what they have accomplished. I know that the students and families appreciate the time and the structure because by the fourth conference each school year, there is nearly 95 percent participation with several hundred people filling our school cafeteria on a student-led conference evening. They are also significant because most of my students and their families do not have an academic background. Therefore, discourse around student work and the standards they are trying to achieve is often absent. Because the conferences begin by following a script, and because the students have done role-playing in our class prior to the first conference, students and their families are more comfortable with the process. Students are also able to conduct the conference in their home language, which also makes families better able to participate.

Analysis and Reflection: How Has What You Have Described Had an Impact on Students' Learning?

With student-led conferences, no one hides. Grades are not about what the teacher puts in the roll book, they are about what the student does in school. Students use evidence from their portfolios to document their accomplishments. Because students know early in the school year that there will be an audience for their work, they pay more attention to what they do. I know this is true because even for underperforming students, there is a significant improvement in their participation, completion, and quality of work between conferences. Sometimes my students report their parents have reduced the number of chores they require so they can do their schoolwork—a serious issue in a community where children are expected to contribute to the family income or care for younger siblings. Sometimes students complain because their parents begin to monitor TV and computer use more closely. By the fourth conference, at the end of the year, nearly all students and their families are in attendance. It's a celebration of student achievement. All in all, everyone wins. One year, a parent gave me a copy of the video *Mr. Holland's Opus* because of the impact I had on his son. I wish I could say that every student successfully passes from my ninth-grade classes, but that is not so. Most do meet the standards, and our tenth-grade teachers always tell me that my students are better prepared than are the students from most of the other teachers.

Documentation included copies of photos of a room filled with students and families, a short letter from a parent, and part of a reflection extracted from a student portfolio addressing how these conferences changed his academic life.

Discussion

The preceding activity meets the criteria for a documented accomplishment. It certainly contributed to student learning. It engaged parents as partners in their children's learning by helping them to understand the nature of a portfolio, the district standards, and how they could assist their children academically. There was interaction, not just direction from the teacher to the parents. The candidate continued learning by attending a professional conference and reading books to improve her practice.

As a side note, this was one of my activities, probably the most effective strategy I ever used. It impacted how I conducted class, instilled reflective practice for my students, engaged the parents, and much more. And it was easy to do, actually making my job as an English Language Arts teacher much less time-consuming. For the last 6 years of my teaching career, I held these conferences. With all of those hundreds of students, I had only one disagreement with a parent about a student's final grade. The students learned that they earned their grades through meeting the standards. What a valuable lesson for them: focused, consistent effort leads to rewards. Now as a teacher of adults, I continue to hold my students' portfolios (NB candidates) up to examination by others, and I continue to improve my practice along the way.

WRITING PRACTICE

Now it's time for you to practice writing one accomplishment for this entry. Your sample doesn't have to meet all three categories, but it might.

- ☐ Select one of the activities you've listed on the activity pages. Type your response in the required format so you will begin to get a sense of how much you can say on a page. All of the entries have maximum page allowances, which the assessors will not read beyond.
- ☐ Description—answer this question: *What is the nature of this accomplishment?* The assessors will know nothing about you except for what they read in your Contextual Information Sheet. You must be specific, providing enough detail for the activity to come alive. Keep in mind, however, that you have only 10 pages for commentary in which to document a maximum of eight accomplishments. During the drafting stages, don't worry about the length. You'll have time to select the most meaningful accomplishments and revise your writing later.
- ☐ Analysis and reflection: *Why is this accomplishment significant?* Your accomplishment doesn't have to be original; mine wasn't. It does have to be effective and have significance in your teaching context. To do this well, you need to understand your context (completing the Contextual Information Sheet is helpful in informing you, as well as the assessor, about your context) and construct activities that address the challenges

of your teaching environment. It is nearly impossible, and unnecessary, to separate analysis from reflection. When we think about what the activity means, it is intricately connected to why it matters.

☐ More analysis and reflection: *How has what you have described had an impact on students' learning?* You don't have to provide test scores, although you may. You can also use anecdotal commentary. The documentation you provide as evidence should directly relate to what you have described. Direct quotes are always powerful.

☐ With your cohort group, using the Reflective Conversation sentence starters and the Looking at Teachers' Work protocol, if you find them helpful, critique and comment on one another's drafts.

Don't expect one activity to meet the criterion of *clear, consistent, and convincing* evidence of having met the standards. The assessors score the entry in its entirety. What's important is that you have made an impact, that you continue to grow and learn, that you open your practice to families and the greater community, and that you are an active member of a professional community.

When you have completed your initial descriptions and analysis of the activities for this entry, write a two-page reflective summary that examines the patterns you see emerging and identifies plans for the future. You can't write the reflection until you've drafted the entire entry. It is only as you prepare your reflection that you'll be able to make final choices, cutting those activities of least impact or that were isolated events that may have impacted your students but didn't leave an impression on you.

For example, after reviewing the activities I had described in preparation for writing the reflective summary, I recognized two major themes. The first was that I stressed personal responsibility—for teachers, for parents, and most definitely for students. Student-led conferences, for example, were about students acknowledging that their work was the basis for their grades, not the teacher's subjective reaction. The second theme that emerged was my wide-ranging involvement in professional development—my own and that of my colleagues. It was these themes that have continued to guide my career. I now work full-time in the field of professional development. All of this work really took focus during my year of National Board candidacy. The process is powerful.

I have found that many of my colleagues, especially those who teach in secondary schools, have little experience working with families or community members as teaching and learning partners. That was certainly the case for me when I became a National Board candidate. It has since become one of my strongest areas and has greatly impacted my students' learning. Here are some outreach suggestions:

☐ Junior Achievement is a nonprofit, community-based organization that began over eight decades ago. Its mission is to help students learn about our free-enterprise system. It does this through a K–12 curriculum, aligned with state and district content standards. Trained volunteers from the business community come to your school over a period of time, usually 4–8 weeks, and for one period each week they teach age-appropriate facets of our free-enterprise system. There is no cost to the teacher, school, or district. Junior Achievement trains the volunteers and provides the curriculum and all necessary supplies. For more information and to find the Junior Achievement office in your area, consult the website www.ja.org.

☐ Undoubtedly, there are other community-based organizations you could easily tap into. I recently connected with our area Rotary Club, where members have developed an Adopt-a-School program working with one of our local school districts.

☐ *Service learning*, as opposed to community service, matches community needs to the curriculum. Students research their community, identify a need, and then develop a service project to meet that need. Teachers coordinate the curriculum to enrich the experience. For instance, a food drive becomes a service-learning project when a food bank is asked what food it needs. Students learn about nutrition and serving sizes, develop menus, and canvas the community for foodstuffs specific to the menus they've developed. There are opportunities in this project for developing skills in math, writing, telephone communication, nutrition and health, and much more. Students who reach out to help others benefit academically and socially. Service-learning projects provide opportunities for the NB candidate to continue personal learning, work with colleagues across grade levels and disciplines, and engage family and community members in student learning. You hit all three Entry 4 categories with this one. Consult the Internet for more examples of service-learning projects.

☐ Student-led conferences have had the greatest impact on my students' learning and on my teaching than any other strategy I've ever used. Students share their portfolios and evidence of their efforts to meet the designated content standards with their families and other community members. I'm convinced that the description of my student-led conferences, and the accompanying documentation, contributed to my high score on Entry 4. For an easy-to-implement guide to student-led conferences consult my book: *Straight Talk for Today's Teachers: How to Teach so Students Learn*, Heinemann. 2005.

WHAT DOESN'T WORK

I always have the most difficulty explaining to teachers that some of the work they do, especially work they volunteer for, may not be appropriate for this entry. For instance, most sponsorship of student clubs, although absolutely worthwhile, may not fit into documented accomplishments. If you're the Chess Club supervisor and you meet with your students daily at lunch and after school, that still wouldn't work here because it doesn't specifically address any of the three categories: your life as a learner, collaboration, and working with families and community members.

However, if your students wanted a chess club and asked you about it, and you in turn contacted their parents and other teachers and brought those adults in to teach them, and then the students who learned chess from the parents and your colleagues also improved their critical thinking and academic scores, then you might have a documented accomplishment.

Another case that may not apply is work you do on committees, even volunteer work at the school site. Some committees deal primarily with adult issues and rarely affect student learning—even while they may be time-consuming.

Spend your time wisely when you participate beyond your specified classroom assignment, especially during your candidate year. Focus on student learning over adult issues.

Documented Accomplishments Worksheet

Category I: Your work with the families and community of your students (current year)

Category II: Your development as a learner (5 years)

Category III: Your work as a leader/collaborator (5 years)

Accomplishment (Brief)	Significance	Impact on Students	Documentation	Category(ies)

IT'S ABOUT THE WRITING

Yes and no. Writing is a form of communication. Your writing is the main communication between you and the assessors, in addition to student samples, videos and documented evidence. Although you won't lose specific points for misspelled words or grammatical errors, when either gets in the way of the communication, it will have an effect. There is no one style of writing that wins over any other. Say what you need to say, provide specific examples whenever appropriate, and then get out.

Show, don't tell. There is a difference between saying, *"I treat all students equally"* and describing how you do it with, *"Each student has a turn at each class job. We use a work-wheel with all the student's names on it. The wheel is rotated daily, or weekly, thus ensuring each student has an opportunity to complete each job assignment."* The first example tells us that you treat students equitably, but the second example shows us how you do it in ways all assessors can understand. That's what we mean by *show, don't tell.*

Keep the language simple. There are no bonus points for using education jargon. On the contrary, I find that jargon often gets in the way of clear communication. Besides, some jargon is regional, not national, and the assessor may misunderstand your comments. When in doubt, consult the Portfolio-Related Terms included with the portfolio instructions and use the definitions you find there when you choose terms to describe your practice.

Direct references to the standards are unnecessary and can get in the way. I've read portfolio entries in which the candidate says, "This is in accordance with Standard VI, Meaningful Applications of Knowledge." Those references take up valuable space and are a distraction. Besides, the assessors will read beyond your references, searching for the evidence of the standard in your practice. It's not what you tell them you do, it's what you show the assessors through examples and student work, your videos, and your documented accomplishments that counts. This is another case of show, don't tell. If you are addressing the standards in your practice, in the work you assign your students, in how you provide feedback, and in the strategies you select, the assessors will find the standards without you pointing them out.

Likewise, you don't have to make specific references to research you have read, unless your teaching decisions are based on it. Providing a litany of researchers and their pet theories doesn't impress anyone. Stating Vygotsky's Zone of Proximal Development, then teaching way above the students' current ability level doesn't speak well of you. On the other hand, knowing what the students already know and then pitching your lesson to just a bit above their level—enough to challenge them but not enough to discourage them—is evidence of accomplished teaching even if you don't know, or don't state, that it's related to Vygotsky's Zone of Proximal Development. It is the same as if you describe the context of your teaching and then fail to address your students' relevant characteristics when you set instructional goals or select strategies to help students reach those goals.

Don't go out of your way to quote theory you don't apply in your practice. However, if it is natural for you to make reference to researchers or theories, do so when applicable. Be real. Be yourself. This is all about adding value to your students' lives—it is not about razzle-dazzle or an academic treatise.

In the current portfolio instructions, the National Board gives some examples of descriptive, analytical, and reflective writing. I'm sorry to say I don't think the examples are very well done, nor do I know if the NB will change them in subsequent years. The NB does state that the examples given are unscored. Therefore, don't give them an inordinate amount of weight. Your cohort group is more likely to help you improve your writing through questioning techniques than you'll accomplish by mimicking styles found in the instructions. Read more about how to work with cohort groups in the next chapter.

I'm always reluctant to share high-scoring portfolio entries, even my own, with my candidate groups. On the one hand, everyone benefits from seeing some modeling. On the other hand, some candidates think they have to write their entries in the same style as other entries they've read. One way around this is to read scored portfolio entries only in certificate areas other than your own. In that way you can read some examples, but you won't be tempted to mimic because the content won't apply.

Several websites feature candidate portfolios, chat rooms, and other tips. Personally, I encourage my candidates to avoid them. Too much of the information is inaccurate or outdated. Sometimes a candidate who didn't achieve uses a chat room to rant about the unfair assessment practices and bias of the National Board. Trust your practice. If you're teaching at an accomplished level, and you communicate that clearly and convincingly, you'll achieve National Board certification.

As I stated in the introduction, this workbook is not intended to be a test-prep course. Just as there isn't one way to teach all students, there isn't one way to complete the portfolio entries successfully. You can, however, follow the instructions, address the standards, and provide *clear, convincing,* and *consistent* evidence of student accomplishment.

Cream rises to the top, and accomplished teachers achieve certification.

I recommend that you set up four text documents on your computer, one for each entry. Set the page defaults (1-inch margins top/bottom/left/right). Set for double spacing, 12 point Times New Roman font. In the header type *Entry 1* followed by the title of the entry to the left and your candidate ID number to the right. In the footer, insert automatic page numbers.

Now, return to the portfolio instructions for Entry 1. Using bold-faced text, type the prompts directly onto the page you just set up. Next to the prompt, type the recommended number of pages and the maximum page limit. You're now ready to write your entry. Answer each prompt exactly as asked. When you have finished drafting (maybe months from now), and your cohort group has had the opportunity to comment upon your entry, you can remove the prompts. Voila! A completed entry.

16 COLLABORATION AND COHORT GROUPS

If you've come this far, you've most likely decided this is the year you're going to work toward achieving National Board certification. Congratulations. You're already in the top 1 percent of the teaching profession. Now, let's talk about working smarter, not harder. Open up your classroom doors and let your colleagues in.

The National Board encourages collaboration. The stipulation is that the work you submit must be the direct result of your teaching, even if you wrote lesson plans with your colleagues, did team teaching for part of your day, or planned and executed parent workshops together. Do include information about your collaboration in your entry. If you team teach all of the time, that is certainly part of your contextual information and your instructional context. If you are on a loosely structured team, say so. Our work does not have to be original, it just has to be effective for our students. Remember, the work you submit is yours alone.

Many NB candidates go it alone, but I don't have any official statistics on how many are successful. I do know, from my extensive experience, that candidates who work in dedicated cohort groups have a significantly higher chance of achieving certification and enjoy the process much more. I waited nearly 2 years from the time I first became interested in certification until I was able to entice some colleagues to join me in this professional endeavor. I know that the experience was richer because I shared it with others. Of our original group of 18, 50 percent certified the first year at a time when the certification rate nationally was hovering under 35 percent, and all but one certified on the second attempt. More important, we learned so much from one another during the months we worked together. An excitement and energy develop among dedicated teachers working on a common goal that is rarely matched in the faculty lounge or any other professional setting.

The candidate support program I direct meets for four or five consecutive days during the summer months to begin the NB process, then monthly, and then semimonthly as a pre-K–12 facilitated group. Candidates are strongly encouraged to meet with small (4–6 members) cohort groups in between the facilitated meetings. These are the colleagues who will read each of your entries, nurture you as you probe your practice, encourage you when you feel overwhelmed, and help you stick to the timeline. By the end of the NB process, you will have bonded. (The children of two of my

candidates who participated in the same cohort group met and married!)
Teachers who work collaboratively vow they will never work in isolation
again. I like to think I'm important to their success, and in some ways I am,
but it's the cohort group that provides the greatest support.

FORMING A SUCCESSFUL COHORT GROUP

Eight years ago, when I began this work, I thought all I needed to do was
put four teachers around a table and they would immediately be collaborative. (Isn't that what we often do in our classrooms?) Some groups did work
well from the outset, but most didn't. Since then I always take time to teach
collaborative practices. Although I'm working with teachers, all of these
practices can move into the classroom. Here's a step-by-step method that
works well when forming working groups.

First, begin with a personal learning reflection.

Instructions

Write five endings for this sentence:
I learn best when . . .
-
-
-
-
-

Now write five endings for this sentence:
I don't learn well when . . .
-
-
-
-
-

Form a cohort group with others who share similar learning styles or who are flexible enough to adapt to one another. If one person learns best with loud music blasting and you demand absolute quiet, you're probably not a good match. In addition to learning style you may want to consider colleagues who are working on the same certificate, who teach at the same school or a school nearby, who live near you, who like to meet on Saturday mornings, or who will never meet on Saturday mornings, for instance. Once you've gathered agreeable colleagues, take the time to establish some group norms.

Instructions

Determine the five norms your group believes are essential for a strong professional learning community. Engage in a discussion about each member's beliefs, then write down what you agree to. (For the classroom, what would happen if instead of class rules you and your students established classroom norms essential for a learning community and for promoting academic success?)

SUGGESTED SIMPLE RULES FOR EFFECTIVE COHORT GROUPS

1. Agree to a regularly scheduled meeting place and time.
2. Be prompt—arrive on time.
3. Be prepared with the assignment the group agreed upon at the previous session. Use the timeline as a guide.
4. Be productive—stay focused on the issue(s) addressed during each cohort meeting. Don't waste time whining about things you can't control. Focus on your teaching and student learning.
5. Be polite and respectful of one another's feelings, teaching context, and challenges.
6. Stay committed to one another. You're in this for the long haul.

LOOKING AT TEACHERS' WORK

During your period of candidacy, especially working in small cohort groups, you'll be sharing your writing, your videos, your students' work, your strengths, and your weaknesses. For many candidates, this is the first time they have worked so intimately with colleagues. Sharing involves risk taking. The portfolio entries are not about a teacher saying "I do this" or "I do that in my classroom," but about examining what the students do and accomplish as a result of what the teacher does.

We share and learn best in a physically and emotionally safe atmosphere. Teachers and students are more willing to take intellectual risks when they know their audience is committed to listening in an active and respectful manner. What follows is a guide for promoting thoughtful, safe questioning of one another's practice, while helping to uncover and recover what is happening in our classrooms and with our students. Remember, the techniques that work well with teachers work equally well with students.

First, the basics: begin with *positive presuppositions*:

☐ Assume the teachers sharing work have good intentions in the work they do with students and others.

☐ Carefully pose the questions you ask to assure there are no hidden negatives.

  • Example: There's a difference between asking: *What were you thinking when you did that?* and *What was your rationale/reasons for choosing that strategy with this lesson?*

☐ Avoid causing your colleagues to shut down.

Reflective Conversation

Reflective conversation can do the following:

☐ Serve as effective sentence starters

☐ Focus us on the work before us, not the personality of the presenter

☐ Be sensitive to others' vulnerabilities

☐ Be helpful in promoting safe learning environments, although they are not magic

☐ Be altered or abandoned as the group members become more comfortable with one another

I've learned all of the preceding techniques from a variety of sources, some from the National Board training, much from practice, reflection, and more practice. Although I would like to give credit where it is due, I'm not sure I could assign any one idea to any one original source. Therefore, I wish to publicly acknowledge the many colleagues who have contributed to my own learning, to the National Board, and to WestEd and other education groups, formal and informal.

Reflective Conversations

The reflective conversation questions and statements that follow, work especially well for any group, teachers or students, examining one another's writing or critiquing a video, an artwork, or any product worth examining to learn how and what to improve. I suggest that members of the group read the sentence starters aloud before you begin using them. It may seem a little artificial, but it is a way to exercise the tongue and get it used to using the sentence starters. These sentence starters will actually help you stay away from some of the pitfalls I describe later. These are reflective conversation words and phrases (use as sentence starters):

PARAPHRASING

So . . .

In other words . . .

What I'm hearing then . . .

What I hear you saying . . .

From what I hear you say . . .

I'm hearing many things . . .

As I listen to you, I'm hearing . . .

Paraphrasing is the following:

- ☐ A restatement by the listener of what he or she understood
- ☐ Not an alteration of the speaker's intent
- ☐ A summary of what the listener heard
- ☐ A prompt for the speaker to restate or explain if the listener needs more clarification

CLARIFYING

Would you tell me a little more about . . . ?

Let me see if I understand . . .

I'd be interested in hearing more about . . .

It'd help me understand if you'd give me an example of . . .

So, are you saying/suggesting . . . ?

Tell me what you mean when you . . .

Tell me how that idea is like (different from) . . .

To what extent . . . ?

I'm curious to know more about . . .
I'm intrigued by . . .
I'm interested in . . .
I wonder . . .

Probing and clarifying questions

- [ ] Are posed when the audience doesn't understand
- [ ] Are used when the audience needs more information
- [ ] Help speakers extend the information
- [ ] Help us to interpret our practice more deeply

MEDIATIONAL

What's another way you might . . . ?
What would it look like if . . . ?
What do you think would happen if . . . ?
How was . . . different from (like) . . . ?
What sort of an impact do you think . . . ?
What criteria do you use to . . . ?
When have you done something like . . . before?
What do you think . . . ?
How did you decide . . . (come to that conclusion)?
What might you see happening in your classroom if . . . ?

We pose questions to do the following:

- [ ] Promote analytical and reflective thinking
- [ ] Encourage articulation of thoughts
- [ ] Uncover things we know and things we don't know
- [ ] Push ourselves to explore our learning more deeply

WORKING WITH THE COHORT GROUP

Okay, you've formed your cohort, you've established your group norms, and now you're ready to work. Much of the work you do together this year will be examining your written portfolio entries and viewing and analyzing one another's videotapes. You can use many protocols to examine one another's entries and tapes. Most groups benefit from beginning with a structured protocol while they are getting used to working with one another, and then abandoning it once trust is established. Check out the Internet for other examples, or use the one included in this workbook—it works. (Don't forget, it works very well with student groups also.)

LOOKING AT TEACHERS' WORK—A PROTOCOL

For this protocol, use the reflective conversation sentence starters. Take a few minutes with your cohort group to read aloud the reflective conversation questions and statements so they are fresh in your mind. Remember as you examine one another's work to *presume good intentions*. The purpose is to provide constructive feedback without causing others to shut down or become defensive. For ease of explanation, I've used a draft of a portfolio entry as the focus of the task. You can easily substitute a video or student work. Talking about and collectively analyzing student work is excellent preparation for writing the portfolio entries.

The tuning protocol, a process for reflection on teacher and student work, is loosely adapted from the work of the Coalition of Essential Schools. The time allotments indicated are suggestions only. The protocol is a recommendation only, not mandatory.

The team consists of a facilitator, presenting teacher, and responding teachers/others. Groups of four are ideal, five is okay, but when the group is larger, it is not as efficient.

The protocol proceeds as follows:

1. Introduction (3 minutes): Facilitator briefly introduces the protocol goals, norms, and agenda.
2. Teacher presentation (10 minutes): Presenter describes the context for the student work (something about the class and its challenges, the instructional goals, the scoring rubric, the strategies used, what came before and after) and presents samples of student work. Presenting teacher may request specific feedback about one or more aspects of the lesson and/or student work.
3. Clarifying questions: (5–10 minutes): See the Reflective Conversations sentence starters included above. Each person in the group may ask one or more clarifying questions. The presenting teacher clarifies and makes note of what was unclear.

4. **Pause (2–3 minutes):** Participants pause to reflect on what feedback they want to give the presenting teacher—both warm and constructive feedback.

5. **Warm comments and constructive feedback (10–15 minutes):** Participants engage in a discussion with one another while the presenting teacher listens *silently*. Facilitator may remind participants of the presenting teacher's focus or any requests for feedback the presenting teacher expressed earlier.

6. **Reflection/response (10–15 minutes):** Presenting teacher reflects on and responds to comments he or she chooses. Participants are silent. Facilitator may clarify.

7. **Debrief (5–10 minutes):** Beginning with the presenting teacher, each participant makes a final comment about the content or the process. Facilitator wraps up.

GUIDELINES FOR FACILITATORS

1. Be assertive about keeping time. Don't let one participant monopolize.

2. Be protective of presenting teachers. Try to determine just how tough your presenter wants the feedback to be. Teachers have different comfort levels with public work.

3. Be provocative of substantive discourse. There is no benefit if all the participants just make general comments.

NORMS FOR PARTICIPANTS

1. Be respectful of presenting teachers. By making their work public, teachers are exposing themselves to the kinds of critiques they may not be used to. Inappropriate comments or questions should be recast or withdrawn.

2. Contribute to substantive discourse. Without constructive comments, no one benefits.

3. Be appreciative of the facilitator's role about keeping time and following the norms.

Repeat the protocol for each presenting teacher. It's a good rule of thumb to state at the onset of the meeting how much total time is available; two hours may be available for most meetings. Divide the number of teachers seeking feedback into the total available time so each member is assured of equal time. Adjust protocol accordingly.

Avoid the pitfalls of trying to solve teaching problems, change the teaching, or suggesting other strategies to use for the lesson. Those are great items to discuss at another time or later during the meeting. For this part of the group session, it's important to focus on what the candidate wrote and the content of the draft. Did the entry address the standards? Did the candidate follow the instructions? Was this work representative of accomplished teaching? Although the candidate always makes the final decision about what should or should not be included, feedback from the group is invaluable. If all are saying the same thing about clarity, choice, or anything else, it's worth listening. I've never had a candidate tell me that he or she didn't benefit from working with the group.

Note: This protocol is like a script. Use it if it assists you in accomplishing the goal—to clearly document your teaching practice in response to the entry prompts. Discard the protocol in part or in whole if you find that it hampers the process rather than aiding it, but try it a few times before abandoning it—it works.

It is really important to remember that when you send your portfolio to the board, you won't have the luxury of sitting on the assessor's shoulder and clarifying or adding to anything you've written. The portfolio entry stands alone. Here's why having an audience beyond yourself, an audience of candidates who have a personal investment in your success as you have in theirs, is so valuable. Pretend that each member of your cohort group represents an assessor. What each understands, the assessor will most likely understand. What you write and how clearly and fully you analyze your teaching practices will help the assessor accurately score your entry. Make it easy. Write clearly and concisely, follow the instructions, respond to the guiding questions, address the standards, and include all the required forms, evidence, and documents.

 # ASSESSMENT CENTER EXERCISES

In addition to the four portfolio entries, each candidate must complete six assessment center exams of 30 minutes duration each. Unless the candidate makes arrangements for special accommodations, all of these exams are done on the same day at one of hundreds of computer testing centers located around the country. The candidate has a window in which to schedule an appointment and take the exams. Consult the NB website for dates. The exams may not be scheduled, however, until all the fees have been paid. Once candidates take the exams, even if they have not yet submitted their portfolios, the NB fees are nonrefundable.

I strongly suggest, as do many of my colleagues who support candidates, that you complete your portfolio entries before taking the assessment exams. Most candidates feel more confident writing about student learning and their own teaching after they have spent several months on their portfolio entries.

Unlike the portfolio entries, which have many commonalities, the assessments are certificate-specific, stressing content knowledge. Some exams require candidates to analyze student work samples and suggest next steps for continued student achievement. Others test for deep levels of knowledge in specific disciplines. Most responses are typed directly on the computer, but several, for world language and music for example, have aural components. Some math and science notation may be done on paper and submitted to the NB by the testing center along with your computerized responses.

Candidates have reported that their typing skills impacted their test results. You have only 30 minutes for each exam. If you are still a two-finger typist, you will be at a disadvantage. Practice, practice, practice keyboarding. Here's another reason for submitting the portfolio first: you'll have spent months typing and will most likely have improved your skill. Do complete the online tutorial to become better acquainted with the computer directions. You want this experience to be about teaching, not about computer skills, or a lack thereof.

Together, the six exams are worth only 40 percent of the total NB score. If you do not achieve certification on the first attempt, you can elect to redo any of the exams on which you have scored poorly. You will not have to redo all of the exams.

It is valuable to begin preparation for the assessment center portion of the National Board assessment while you are working on your portfolio entries. The work you complete for your portfolio will help prepare you for the assessment center, and studying for the assessment center will enhance your portfolio entries. Go to NBPTS Assessment Center Orientation (online) at www.nbpts.org/candidates/acob to view exercise descriptions for your certificate. The following suggestions will prepare you for a successful assessment center experience.

- ☐ Download and review the six assessment center overviews (these are also in the Scoring Guide, which you may have already downloaded).
- ☐ Read levels 4 and 3 in the rubrics for each of the assessment center exercises. Rubric level 4 is your target.
- ☐ For each certificate there are two *retired* assessment center prompts; these are at the end of your Scoring Guide.
- ☐ Although your actual prompts will be different, they will have a similar structure.
- ☐ Consult the rubric for clues as to what the exercise will look like and what you will be asked to do: identify, discuss, analyze, find errors, and so forth.
  - Consider which action words ask for short, to-the-point answers and which require longer, more in-depth responses.
- ☐ Use the retired prompts for timed written responses. You may also write some possible prompts and have your certificate-alike colleagues write some prompts also, then respond to them in timed tests approximating the test site conditions as closely as possible—30 minutes uninterrupted at a computer station. Some candidates have test phobia. If you fall into this category, practicing in timed tests will reduce test anxiety.
  - Use the Scoring Guide rubric to judge the quality of your responses objectively.
- ☐ Complete the assessment center tutorial before going to the assessment center. You can find the tutorial at www.nbpts.org/candidates/tutorial.cfm.

At the assessment center (thanks to my colleagues at WestEd, San Francisco for this) do the following:

- [ ] Read through all of the prompts in the 30-minute question first; there are sometimes two, three, or four different prompts within a single question.

- [ ] Budget time for each question—if there are three prompts consider using 10 minutes per prompt—so that you have a chance to respond fully.

- [ ] Respond to each subsection with your main points and then go back and fill in more detail later if there is time. This way, your main ideas will be submitted for each question instead of you overspending time on a single prompt and shortchanging the others.

- [ ] Start writing and keep writing. If you get stumped, restart by restating the question as your response; this might jog your memory—just to get your fingers moving.

- [ ] Your answers do not have to be in paragraph or prose form. It is okay to use bulleted statements when you can. Your job is to answer the questions posed in each prompt.

- [ ] Be sure to answer directly the prompt as stated. For example, if the prompt asks you to state the learning goals and describe what you would do to help a student to reach those goals, don't forget to actually state the learning goals in very specific terms.

- [ ] You will only have access to one exam at a time. When you leave one exam to go to the next, you cannot return to the prior exam. Use the entire 30 minutes before closing one exam and opening another. Unused time does not carry forward, it's lost forever.

Relax. If you know your content area, if you've spent months analyzing your student work, you'll be fine. They're just tests. Your students take tests all the time and they manage; you can also.

SCORING

Standards-based instruction begins with the standards against which the student, or in the case of the National Board, the candidate will be assessed. The standards are followed by clear instructions for demonstrating accomplishment and a scoring guide by which the student's performance or candidate's entry will be scored. National Board certification is standards-based performance assessment of the highest caliber. Nothing is hidden, nothing is left to chance. Everyone knows up front what is expected and how to meet those expectations. This is as close to objective scoring as you are likely to find. Classroom teachers should provide this same structure for students: the standards to be addressed; clear, explicit instructions that allow for differentiated responses; and a scoring guide or rubric by which the student's efforts will be measured.

For each entry, the National Board includes a section called "How Will My Response Be Scored" that includes a level-4 scoring rubric. Study it. Use the rubric when you plan your entry. Use it again when you're writing your responses to the prompts. And refer to it a third time when you have completed your draft and you're self-scoring or scoring with your cohort group. Be objective. Only when you've written your complete written commentary and included your student work or video or the evidence of your documented accomplishments are you or your cohort group able to score the entry. The assessors will score only what you submit in the envelope, your written analysis, videos, student work and evidence. You can't verbally add anything later because you won't be sitting with the assessors explaining what you really meant.

For the first several years I worked with National Board portfolios, I completely missed their careful choice of the word *response*. In my mind, *response* was interchangeable with *answer,* but it isn't. Whereas *answers* tend to be specific, limited, and generally known in advance, *responses* are open-ended and filled with possibilities. The NB asks you to respond to the prompts.

Each performance, portfolio entry, or assessment center exam is scored independently on a 0.75 to 4.25 score scale as follows:

THE SCORE SCALE

0.75 1.00 1.25	1.75 2.00 2.25	2.75 3.00 3.25	3.75 4.00 4.25
The 1 Family	The 2 Family	The 3 Family	The 4 Family

The scoring instrument is a modified four-point score scale. Performances are assigned a whole number score (1, 2, 3, or 4) and then, if appropriate, the whole number score is augmented with a plus or minus. Plus and minus scores are represented numerically as an increment or decrement of 0.25 from the whole number score. For example, a 1+ is equivalent to a 1.25, a 3– is equivalent to a 2.75. Scores can range from 0.75 to 4.25.

Assessors classify performances into the score category that best fits the performance, and then they may shade the score up or down to reflect a strong or weak performance in that category. Score families are distinct from one another; entries must ultimately be assigned to one family or another, not in between.

To achieve certification the candidate must accumulate 275 points out of a possible 400 (actually, it's possible, but highly unlikely, to score 425). Portfolio entries and assessment exercises are weighted. Entries 1, 2, and 3 are each worth 16 percent of the total score. Entry 4, Documented Accomplishments, is worth 12 percent. Each assessment center exam is worth 6.67 percent. The total portfolio counts for 60 percent of the final grade, the assessment center only 40 percent. Put your effort where you'll get the greatest payoff. Scores are cumulative. It is possible to receive a low score on one entry or one test but still achieve certification because another entry or test scored high.

Candidates who do not achieve certification on the first attempt (notice I don't use the words *pass* or *fail* because everyone who completes is a winner—actually, everyone who attempts is a winner) may bank their scores for 24 months. Candidates then determine which entries or exams they want to retake. If you retake a portfolio entry, it is the same one you did before, only with your current students. If the banking candidate elects to redo an assessment center exam, he or she will have a new exam in the same category as the original one, but not the same exact prompt. The score from a retake entry or exam automatically replaces the original score, even if it is lower. About half of all candidates who don't achieve on the first attempt do achieve on the second attempt. Few candidates drop out of the process.

Forget it, there isn't any. This is the most thoughtful, the most fair scoring process I have ever been associated with, and I've scored state exams, Disney teacher awards, the Skirball National Essay contest, and more. Assessors are classroom teachers in your certificate area. They receive 4 days of intensive training to rid themselves of any personal biases that may affect scoring. They study the standards, and then they study the standards again. They calibrate the entry they will be scoring, and they score the same entry for an entire 2- to 3-week period. They read so thoroughly, they can usually score only about eight candidates' entries a day. This is a time-consuming, expensive assessment process, and that's how your NB fees are spent. Although the National Board has a method whereby you can contest your score, I don't know anyone who has successfully done so. I have, however, worked with a number of banking candidates who, upon careful and objective rereading of their entries, felt they could have written more thoroughly or more clearly about their classroom practice and did so on their retake entry.

Save yourself some anxiety and possible disappointment by scoring your entries before you submit them. Give yourself plenty of time by completing your drafted entries at least several weeks before the portfolio due date. If your drafted entry doesn't receive a high score from your own or your cohort's scoring, consider revision.

You may use one or both of the scoring matrixes included here when you practice scoring your entries. Duplicate them as needed.

PORTFOLIO SCORING MATRIX

CERTIFICATE: _____

Directions: In the left column enter the title of each of the standards for your certificate. In each of the next four columns, mark an X for each standard you are to address in the entry. Using a different color, read your response to each entry and mark an X each time you find evidence of the standard. You're accomplished if you find clear, consistent, and convincing evidence in your response for each required standard.

STANDARD	ENTRY 1	ENTRY 2	ENTRY 3	ENTRY 4
I.				
II.				
III.				
IV.				
V.				
VI.				
VII.				
VIII.				
IX.				
X.				
XI.				
XII.				
XIII.				
XIV.				
XV.				

SCORING YOUR ENTRY—TAKE TWO

Directions: In the left column enter the key points for each of the standards that apply to this entry. You'll need to make several copies of this page. Carefully read your portfolio entry response. Mark an X each time you find evidence you have addressed this standard. Record the nature of the evidence. Look for *clear, consistent,* and *convincing* evidence. For an even more accurate assessment, ask members of your cohort group to score your portfolio entry. If they find the evidence, there is a good chance the assessor will also. If they don't find *clear, consistent,* and *convincing* evidence, consider revising your entry.

STANDARD — KEY POINTS	EVIDENCE (BE SPECIFIC. SHOW, DON'T TELL.)

19   Time Management

Beginning with the 2004–2005 candidate-year, National Board portfolios are all due in the spring on March 31, 2005, this year. (This date may vary slightly from year to year.) Candidates may use evidence from 12 months prior to the portfolio due date—even if it overlaps two school years. The exams must be completed by June following the portfolio due date. An additional 24 months is allowed for retake entries, if needed.

Because you can access the portfolio instructions and standards prior to applying for candidacy, it is strongly recommended that you take the time to study both documents (use this workbook as a guide) prior to sending your $300 nonrefundable application fee. You can begin working on your entries prior to making your official application. Once you've begun analyzing your practice and determining how much time you'll need to complete the board requirements successfully, you are in a better position to decide whether this is the right time for you to attempt certification. You may find, as do some of the teachers who work with me, that an additional 6 months or year of preparation, prior to submitting your official application, will better prepare you for this rigorous, high-stakes assessment process. Or you may be ready to go immediately!

The following monthly timeline is intended as a guide only. There are several references to working with a cohort group, your colleagues who are working toward board certification along with you. Candidates benefit by working with others. Committed colleagues read the drafts of your entries, offer suggestions when you get stuck, and encourage you when you think about quitting. The portfolio entries and standards are excellent texts about which to have meaningful and productive professional discussions. Take advantage of this process to continue your learning. A discussion about cohort groups appears in Chapter 16.

Perhaps the greatest challenge my candidates face is one of time management. To get the greatest benefit from this professional development process it is necessary to allow sufficient time for analysis, writing, reflection, revision, more analysis, and more reflection. Rushing through the portfolio entries or arriving ill-prepared at the assessment center not only increases your stress level, but also reduces your chances to achieve certification. Plan your time well. Eliminate activities that are not productive or that take a disproportionate amount of energy from you. Disassociate from those people who drain your energy, and increase your time with others who give you energy. Optimistic, "I can do it" colleagues are a joy; whiners are just that, whiners.

Although it's true that at schools, as in other organizations, 20 percent of the people do 80 percent of the work, and you're probably in the 20 percent, your candidacy year is a time for you to be a little selfish. Choose carefully how and where you'll spend your time. The suggested timeline included in this workbook may be a suggested timeline but it's based on 8 years of experience as a candidate and support provider for over a thousand candidates.

The $2,500 in National Board fees is a considerable investment. The fees are used to offset the cost of reading, viewing, and scoring candidate entries. If, even the day before you are scheduled to submit your portfolio entries or sit for the assessment center tests, you decide that you are not ready or that your portfolio does not demonstrate accomplishment, you can withdraw and get a partial refund. Once you submit the portfolio or register to take the assessment center tests, you are an official candidate and your fees are nonrefundable. The withdrawal form is available at the NB website.

The second greatest obstacle candidates face is one of reflective practice. We seldom take the time to sit and think, or stand and think, or drive and think, about what we're doing, how well it went, and whether the students got what you intended. The entire National Board process is very reflective. If you're unable to build in time for reflection, a combination of sit-down-and-think time, driving-to-and-from-work think time, going-for-a-walk think time, or writing-in-a-journal time, there's a strong chance that you won't be successful.

Reflection

Can you find time for the National Board process and still do the things you need to do? There are still only 24 hours in the day. How will you add the National Board work to an already busy schedule? What can you reduce or eliminate? Don't forget to keep some time for personal renewal and rejuvenation. You know the old adage about all work and no play; it applies here as well. Likewise, you may be professionally ready, but family demands are greater if you have small children at home, are caring for a parent or other, have a very long commute to work, or have another combination of inflexible commitments. Because this is a process that requires you to produce a product while you are reflecting and changing your teaching and reading and learning and growing, it takes time.

Work backwards from assessment center final date.

MONTH 1

- ☐ Get (order or download from www.nbpts.org) certificate standards and portfolio instructions.
- ☐ Arrange fee support.
- ☐ Apply online for state subsidy, if available, and other possible scholarships.
- ☐ Consider your personal commitments and adjust accordingly.
- ☐ Study NBPTS standards and instructions.
- ☐ Complete personal inventories and plan to strengthen areas of weakness or challenge.
- ☐ Begin/continue reflective practice. Write in a journal.
- ☐ Complete the portfolio entries—overview for all four entries.
- ☐ Begin Entry 4.
- ☐ Arrange for videotaping equipment.
- ☐ Gather together your professional learning cohort and meet.
- ☐ Establish student portfolios (one method for collecting student work).

MONTH 2

- ☐ Apply online for National Board Certification.
- ☐ Select or continue with your cohort group meetings.
- ☐ Calendar meeting times and places.
- ☐ Examine student work to improve teaching and learning:
  - • Go to www.google.com and go to LASW (Looking at Student Work) for protocols for examining student work.
  - • Practice discussing student work using the reflective conversation sentence starters included in this workbook.
- ☐ Select students (more than required) and possible lessons for entries.
- ☐ Check your entries overview to establish/review your time schedule for entries.
- ☐ Establish/maintain student portfolios.
- ☐ Plan/implement family and community outreach activities.
- ☐ Continue journaling as reflective practice.
- ☐ Videotape one or two classes. Watch with your students. Transcribe.

- ☐ Notify your students/families about what you are doing this year. Ask for their support.
- ☐ Get signed student/adult release forms. Release forms in 14 languages are available without charge from the National Board: 1-800-22TEACH.
- ☐ Share/exchange/write cover letters to go with release forms.
- ☐ Describe the context of your teaching environment. Get data from Dataquest, if available in your state, and from school site. See http://data1.cde.ca.gov/dataquest/, for example.
- ☐ Bring student work to your group for examination and analysis.

MONTH 3

- ☐ Study the Portfolio-Related Terms included with the portfolio instructions.
- ☐ Practice videotaping.
- ☐ Transcribe video while paying careful attention to questioning techniques.
- ☐ Overcome technical difficulties.
- ☐ Analyze what you see in the video. Use analysis guide in Chapter 12.
- ☐ Share with group.
- ☐ Write draft of video entry.
- ☐ Continue journaling as reflective practice.
- ☐ Draft Entry 4. Check for gaps. Plan to fill in gaps.
- ☐ Continue to examine student work to inform instruction.
- ☐ Consider/develop/use rubrics/scoring guides.

MONTH 4

- ☐ Complete penultimate draft of Entry 4.
- ☐ Select/confirm/teach lessons for portfolio entries.
- ☐ Draft second entry.
- ☐ Continue reflective practice.

MONTH 5

- ☐ Complete Entry 4.
- ☐ Complete second entry.
- ☐ Draft last two entries.
- ☐ Share with colleagues.

MONTH 6

☐ Complete drafts of all entries.
☐ Share with colleagues.
☐ Score entries against the standards.
☐ Revise entries.

MONTH 7

☐ Revise/complete entries and compile all documentation.
☐ Edit and proofread.
☐ Fill gaps, if any.
☐ Mail portfolio entries.
☐ Make appointment for assessment center.

MONTHS 8–10

☐ Prepare for assessment center.
☐ Take timed practice tests.
☐ Complete assessment center exercises.
☐ Relax/celebrate/begin waiting.

WAITING FOR SCORES

☐ Celebrate yourself.
☐ Refresh and renew.
☐ Wait.
☐ Wait.
☐ Celebrate your accomplishment.

Before making any further commitments, such as applying to the National Board and sending your application fee, telling your family you are not going to cook for the next year or take out the trash while you're completing your portfolio, take the time for this reflective quiz. Be flexible because the answers may not quite line up with the Leikert scale; but because this is between you and you, and not for research analysis, precision won't matter. Use the following scale to indicate your answers.

1	Absolutely Not
2	Not Likely
3	Maybe
4	Probably
5	Absolutely Can Do

CONSIDERATION		SCALE			
1. I have 200–400 hours of professional time during this year to devote to this process.	1	2	3	4	5
2. I am a self-starter and self-motivated.	1	2	3	4	5
3. I view myself as a teacher who maintains high standards for myself and sets high expectations for my students.	1	2	3	4	5
4. I have examined the five core propositions and completed my personal inventory.	1	2	3	4	5
5. I have examined the standards for my certificate and completed my personal inventory.	1	2	3	4	5
6. I have examined Entries 1, 2, 3, and 4 and can successfully complete each of them.	1	2	3	4	5
7. I can provide evidence (according to the NB definition) of accomplished teaching.	1	2	3	4	5
8. I have significant evidence of my documented accomplishments available in accordance with Entry 4.	1	2	3	4	5
9. I regularly reflect upon and modify my teaching practices.	1	2	3	4	5
10. I work well with colleagues.	1	2	3	4	5
11. I look forward to sharing and discussing my students' work.	1	2	3	4	5
12. I welcome the comments of other teachers about my written entries.	1	2	3	4	5
13. I welcome the comments of other teachers about my practice.	1	2	3	4	5
14. I look forward to sharing my classroom videos with my cohort group.	1	2	3	4	5

CONSIDERATION	SCALE				
15. I can attend scheduled after-school monthly meetings (or when they are scheduled).	1	2	3	4	5
16. I can meet on a regular basis with my cohort group.	1	2	3	4	5
17. I can travel, if necessary, to meetings in various parts of the city.	1	2	3	4	5
18. I can attend workshops, if necessary, to deepen my knowledge base.	1	2	3	4	5
19. My family/friends will act as a support system for me.	1	2	3	4	5
20. I can limit my personal activities to provide the time I will need.	1	2	3	4	5
21. My current school administration will support my candidacy (emotional support, video equipment, release time, etc.).	1	2	3	4	5
22. I can say no when asked to join still another school committee or chair another school function.	1	2	3	4	5
23. I am computer literate and have e-mail and Internet access.	1	2	3	4	5
24. I can arrange to pay the NB fees myself, if necessary.	1	2	3	4	5
25. I am not a procrastinator. I can follow the suggested timeline or create one I will follow.	1	2	3	4	5
26. I am already an accomplished teacher.	1	2	3	4	5

Now add up your scores. If you're at 65 or below, you should most likely wait a while. In the 65–80 range, it doesn't sound like you have a strong commitment, yet. If your score is 80–100, you're looking good. Over 100, what are you waiting for?

Of course, this is a very nonscientific survey. Just something some friends and I came up with. Thanks to Diana Cotter of Los Angeles Unified and the hundreds of teachers who have shared these questions with me.

Reflection

This is it. You are beginning the National Board process, approximately 10 months of describing, analyzing, and reflecting on your teaching practice. Where are you going to find the time? How are you going to do it all? What activities are you planning to reduce or cut out? How will you organize your time? Your space for working? What scares you? Excites you? What are your burning concerns, if any?

PACKING AND SHIPPING

The packing and shipping instructions are included in the portfolio instructions. The bar-coded labels arrive with your box, after your application fee is processed. You will return the completed entries, including the videos, in the envelopes and in the same box you received many months before. The instructions tell you exactly how and where to place the bar codes, how to complete and organize the forms, and what to put where. Follow the directions.

Do . . .

- ☐ Meet or beat the due date.
- ☐ Read and follow all of the instructions—exactly.
- ☐ Make and keep copies of everything, including computer backups along the way—nothing will be returned to you.
- ☐ Celebrate—you did it!

Don't . . .

- ☐ Discard the box.
- ☐ Wait until the last minute and then rush to find a FedEx shipper.
- ☐ Have a packing party. You might get your papers mixed with someone else's, and then both of you won't achieve certification. If you must pack with a colleague, pack one box first, remove all copies and other traces of the first candidate's work, then pack the next candidate, then the next.
- ☐ Start thinking about what you could have, should have, would have done—you're done!

REFERENCES

Bransford, J. D., Brown, A. L., et al., Eds. 2000. *How People Learn*. Washington, D.C.: National Academy Press.

Finn, P. J. 1999. *Literacy With an Attitude*. Albany: State University of New York Press.

Johnson, E. B. 2002. *Contextual Teaching and Learning*. Thousand Oaks: Corwin Press, Inc.

Thornburg, D. 2002. *The New Basics: Education and the Future of Work in the Telematic Age*. Alexandria: Association for Supervision and Curriculum Development.

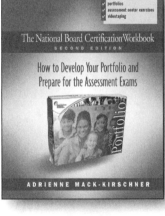